Praise for
Communication the Cleveland Clinic Way

"At our very core, we are people caring for people. In order to excel, we need to make sure our caregivers know how to care. In *Communication the Cleveland Clinic Way*, Boissy and Gilligan provide an incredible how-to care guide as their team took on the challenge of ensuring empathy in over 5,000 caregivers. This book is really a journey that reveals the pitfalls and pearls of such a monumental undertaking and why every health system needs to do the same."

—David Feinberg, MD, MBA, President
and CEO, Geisinger Health System

"Reengaging and enabling physicians in an increasingly challenging work environment, Boissy and Gilligan are spot on. Enhancing communication builds the physician-patient relationship in a way that creates a superior patient experience *and* a superior physician experience."

—Vivian S. Lee, MD, PhD, MBA, CEO,
University of Utah Health Care

"Communicating effectively with patients is not an innate skill, and the emotional detachment we learn in medical training prevents us from building rapport and establishing solid relationships with our patients. Recognizing that there needed to be a better way, this book is a comprehensive road map created by a group of physicians who set out to transform the doctor-patient relationship and build the new gold standard for relationship-centered care. It is a must-read for every clinical provider.

—James Merlino, MD, President and Chief
Medical Officer, Strategic Consulting Division,
Press Ganey and author of *Service Fanatics*

"This book tells the story of a large and remarkably successful institution-wide program on physician communication skills. Told from a variety of perspectives—including senior executives, physician participants, and educators—it describes the important contributions this program is making to quality, strategy, and the professional meaning and well-being of the physician workforce.

Beyond the inspiring story, the book offers a wealth of detail on instructional content and design that will be an enormous resource for others seeking to create their own communication programs. And it describes with great clarity the single most essential feature of a successful program: the informal curriculum or learning environment. We see the intentional effort to treat participants with the same kind of respect and engagement that they are being taught to show to patients."

—Anthony L. Suchman, MD, MA, Senior Consultant,
Relationship Centered Health Care

"Today, external demands and pressures have left many dedicated clinicians and healthcare providers struggling to find meaning in their work. This essential book, drawing upon a deep understanding of human relationships and educational principles, illuminates a pathway by which those who are involved in patient care can develop more effective and satisfying partnerships with their patients, patients' families, and colleagues."

—Walter F. Baile, MD, Director, Program for Interpersonal
Communication and Relationship Enhancement (I*CARE),
University of Texas M. D. Anderson Cancer Center

"Within the context of top-rated clinical and service excellence and the Patients First strategy, leaders at Cleveland Clinic have launched an innovative approach to enhance physicians' human-centered communication skills to nurture the ongoing development of empathetic and compassionate interactions with the patients in their care. This practical yet profoundly transformational approach provides opportunities where physicians can reflect upon communications with their patients and family members, gain insights from dialogue with peers, and receive coaching and mentoring from experts to enhance and build new competencies. In addition, this program provides opportunities for clinicians to focus upon the ultimate purpose of healing not only the body but also the mind and soul of all in their care. And while doing so, many may find greater insight into their own human experience, build more resilience, and enhance or restore the joy in their professional careers. This book is an invaluable asset for all who strive to achieve a human-centered approach to healthcare and superior patient experience."

—Pat Rutherford, MS, RN, Vice President,
Institute for Healthcare Improvement

Communication

the
Cleveland
Clinic Way

How to Drive a Relationship-Centered
Strategy for Superior Patient Experience

EDITED BY

ADRIENNE BOISSY, MD, MA
TIM GILLIGAN, MD, MS

Mc
Graw
Hill
Education

New York   Chicago   San Francisco   Athens   London   Madrid
Mexico City   Milan   New Delhi   Singapore   Sydney   Toronto

1 2 3 4 5 6 7 8 9 0   DOC/DOC   1 2 1 0 9 8 7 6

ISBN   978-0-07-184534-2
MHID   0-07-184534-8

ISBN   978-0-07-184535-9
MHID   0-07-184535-6

R.E.D.E., R.E.D.E. to Communicate, and Communicate with H.E.A.R.T. are trademarks of The Cleveland Clinic Foundation.

Library of Congress Cataloging-in-Publication Data

Names: Boissy, Adrienne, editor. | Gilligan, Timothy, editor.
Title: Communication the Cleveland Clinic way : how to drive a relationship-centered strategy for exceptional patient experience / [edited by] Adrienne Boissy, MD and Timothy Gilligan, MD.
Description: New York : McGraw-Hill Education, [2016]
Identifiers: LCCN 2015051012| ISBN 9780071845342 (hardback) | ISBN 0071845348 (hardback)
Subjects: LCSH: Medical personnel and patient. | Patient-centered health care. | Interpersonal communication. | Physician and patient. | Medical ethics. | BISAC: BUSINESS & ECONOMICS / Business Communication / General.
Classification: LCC R727.3 .C665 2016 | DDC 610.7306/9—dc23 LC record available at http://lccn.loc.gov/2015051012

McGraw-Hill Education books are available at special quantity discounts to use as premiums and sales promotions or for use in corporate training programs. To contact a representative, please e-mail us at bulksales@mheducation.com.

For my boys—
I love you to infinity and beyond

AB

To my patients—
who teach me and give meaning to my work

TG

Contents

Foreword

Healthcare is inherently chaotic. Patients are heterogeneous, so their medical problems are complex and their needs variable. Because of this chaos, clinicians need frameworks and the discipline to use them. Yes, every patient is different, and every interaction unique, but structured approaches to interactions with patients enable clinicians to deliver better care and feel calmer while doing so. Clinicians can focus on connecting with the patient, rather than wondering what they should be doing.

This book describes such a framework, along with powerful insights on how to implement it. Adrienne Boissy and her colleagues at Cleveland Clinic have driven remarkable improvements in the communication skills of caregivers, and they have also provided a superb example of how to build social capital. Although this term is not widely used in healthcare today, it is increasingly relevant as we enter a marketplace driven by competition on value—meeting patients' needs as efficiently as possible. If financial capital refers to the monetary resources that enable organizations to build buildings and accomplish other goals that otherwise would be impossible, social capital describes how relationships within the organization allow it do things it otherwise could not do. Social capital explains how some organizations do a better job at meeting patients' needs and why others fall short even though their personnel are just as hardworking and well trained. In higher-performing organizations, the whole is greater than the sum of its parts; in weaker organizations, the opposite is often the case.

To increase value, clinicians have to work more effectively with each other, and with patients and their families. To do that, organizations have to be able to increase their social capital. University of Chicago sociologist Ronald S. Burt[1] describes two basic ways to do this: brokerage and closure. Brokerage describes how organizations learn, and actually *increase* the variation in how they do things. Closure describes how they *reduce* variation, and achieve consistency in working together in an effective and efficient way.

Organizations need both types of functions, as demonstrated by the work on healthcare communication skills at Cleveland Clinic. The Clinic was wise enough to give the responsibility and a blank slate to Boissy, who was well respected by her colleagues but honest and humble enough to admit that she did not know how to accomplish the goal, so she looked outside of her usual context and enlisted other colleagues with the same openness. They spent a year developing an inventory of what work was going on internally, at other healthcare organizations, and at organizations outside healthcare delivery.

In this brokerage phase, Boissy and her colleagues understood that their work was to learn from others, not start from scratch. To learn, and successfully bring ideas from outside into an organization, information brokers have to create what Burt calls "bridges" over which information can traverse, and "holes" through which the information and new practices can enter. Within any large and complex organization, there are suborganizations, and creating bridges and holes among them is an important function of the learning process.

Organizations that are too inwardly focused are at high risk for missing out on new and better ideas that have developed elsewhere. The temptation is always great in any large and well-regarded organization such as Cleveland Clinic to discount work done elsewhere. Fortunately, the Clinic's leadership was willing to confront data suggesting weak performance and then create the imperative to learn and to improve.

But just learning (idea brokering) is not enough to realize actual improvement; organizations also need "closure," to make the better ways of doing things the new local norm. Here again, Boissy and her team sensed that clinicians need a structured framework for approaching interactions with patients, and that this framework could only be spread via trusted colleagues.

One of my favorite parts of this book is the description by Dr. Edward Benzel, then chair of Neurosurgery, of his initial reaction to the request that he become a trained facilitator for the communications initiative. Benzel's response was to try to get the work assigned to a young woman who had recently been recruited to the neurosurgery group. Boissy and her colleagues knew that the framework they were advancing would spread much faster if well-known and trusted authority figures were pushing it. Benzel relented, as did many of his more senior colleagues, and the Clinic avoided one of the most common mistakes in dissemination of best practices— which is to take the path of least resistance and focus efforts on clinicians who have less influence on their colleagues.

When it comes to making a new and better way of doing things a social norm, the accumulation of social capital blurs into social network science. Here, organizations may benefit from the work of researchers such as Yale's Nicholas Christakis, author of *Connected: The Surprising Power of Our Social Networks and How They Shape Our Lives*.[2] They have shown how values (e.g., good communication being essential to professional excellence) can spread from person to person to person. Financial incentives can capture clinicians' attention briefly, but to achieve real and sustained improvement, social norms must be strong enough to exert peer pressure upon clinicians to be reliably excellent with every single patient.

It is worth noting that the Cleveland Clinic experience demonstrates that brokerage and closure are not two sequential phases. Both must go on continuously and indefinitely. The Clinic has been modifying its program right from the start, and we can expect it to have evolved a year or two from now. The learning will never stop, nor should the work to achieve closure by standardizing best practices.

Thomas H. Lee, MD, MSc
Chief Medical Officer, Press Ganey
Professor of Medicine (part-time), Harvard Medical School
Professor of Health Policy and Management, Harvard School of
    Public Health

Preface

My pager went off before I even made it through the hospital doors. Returning the call, I was greeted with "Hey, good morning. It's Joe in the ER. Your patient in Bed 5 is asking for Dilaudid. I don't want to give it to her, but it's up to you." I didn't know the patient in Bed 5 and communicated that as soon as I met her, I'd be happy to treat her pain with something else. Shortly thereafter, I was rounding on the neurology inpatient service, and the residents told me about a young woman, "the patient in Bed 5," who had been admitted overnight for two months of head pain with innumerable requests for Dilaudid. Their frustration and annoyance were palpable. They described treating the patient with IV steroids, magnesium, Compazine, Toradol, morphine, and Dilaudid in a span of a few hours since her admission, as well as starting prophylactic medications to prevent her head pain. I could see the costs compounding in my head. In addition, she had been admitted to our hospital *for three months* the year prior. I took a deep breath and entered the room.

"Good morning, Ms. Hide. I'm Dr. Boissy, the neurologist in charge of your care while you are here. I'm so sorry you spent the night in the ER and are here."

"Thanks." A somewhat groggy young woman with multiple tattoos rolled onto her back to speak with me. She had her forearm over her eyes and wouldn't look at me.

"I'm wondering if you can tell me about yourself."

"My pain is ten out of ten, mainly on the right side . . ."

"Thank you for telling me. What I meant was about you as a person."

"Oh." She shot me a surprised look as her arm came down from her face. "OK, well, I live at home with my parents. It's not that great because we don't really get along. They don't think anything is wrong with me."

"I'm sorry to hear that."

"It's OK, I'm used to it. I also work as a pharmacy tech."

"That must be interesting. Have you had to miss work because of everything going on?"

"Yeah."

"I bet you miss it. This pain that you're having seems to be really impacting you. Most people have ideas about what's happening with them. What do you think?"

"Well, I think I either have MS (multiple sclerosis) or parasites. I read about them online."

"I'm glad you told me. The good news is I'm an MS specialist, and we can easily check your stools for parasites."

"That's good to hear."

"How are you hoping I can help you?"

"I don't think you're going to fix my pain."

"I think you might be right about that. Sounds like we have been trying a lot of different things without much success."

Fast forward two minutes. "Any history of verbal, physical, or sexual abuse?"

She looks down. "I was raped twice as a teenager. No big deal though. Same thing happened to my best friend, and we worked through it by talking about it with each other."

"Oh my God, I'm sorry to hear that. That must have been awful. How else did you make it through?"

"Just friends."

As I began a general exam, I noted scars along her forearms. "Tell me about these."

She smiled and said, "I used to be a cutter. I haven't done that since my teens."

"Sounds like you suffered a lot in your teens."

"I guess so. I'm OK now."

As the physical exam went on, I noticed a large, deforming scar running up her right arm and into the depths of her gown and right chest wall.

"Tell me about this if you can."

"Last year, I set myself on fire."

In 2009, Cleveland Clinic started a program to improve healthcare communication. When the work started, inpatient patient-satisfaction scores related to doctor communication for all hospitals was in the 24th percentile, and for hospitals with over 1,000 beds, it was in the 46th percentile. Five years later, we were in the 99th percentile. This book tells the story of our journey and our work in the hope that you can learn from our experience and launch your own programs to improve patient experience and reinvigorate clinicians' passion for their work.

In healthcare, communication skills are key. "Never events" such as wrong site surgery, ethics consultations, and cases that reach the physician conduct committee, as well as over 50 percent of complaints or grievances in our ombudsman's office and 72 percent of patient reasons for dissatisfaction with their healthcare providers, are related to ineffective communication. Yet with all this knowledge, doing the work and providing the resources necessary to train clinicians in sufficiently rigorous, comprehensive programs that will result in improved performance remains the exception rather than the rule. Instead, we continue to hold physicians accountable for patient satisfaction scores that they don't particularly care about or understand and ask them to sit at the bedside, smile more, and adopt what look like customer service behaviors. We can do better.

People are drawn to healthcare professions at least in part by a desire to care for the sick and to promote health. The opportunity to serve our fellow humans when they are at their most vulnerable is a sacred privilege. To be the person who has the knowledge and skill to help is a profound and anchoring experience. Customer service skills and scripting will never work for healthcare professionals, for those invested in the care they provide patients. They won't work because our patients don't want to be in the hospital and often face life-and-death issues. Although service excellence absolutely has a role in not adding to the patient and family burden and easing anxiety, the gravity of what our patients face at times must be witnessed honestly. Their suffering deserves a place where it can come out, be acknowledged as a substantial ingredient to their experience of illness and hospitalization, be talked about with people they trust, and be shared with us for a little while. This gesture on the part of our patients to crack the door into their hearts and souls is a gift. This gift sets in motion a mutual respect and emotional connection that fuels a relationship of meaning. And once you have that, you'll never go back to the old way of talking to people.

So why is it that we healthcare professionals sometimes lose track of the humanity of those we are treating? What happened to our antennae for emotional cues from our patients? Why do we sometimes judge them as difficult or drug-seeking or manipulative? Why do patients too often experience their encounters with healthcare as unfeeling and uncaring? Can we in medicine imagine doing better and, if so, what would be the most promising course of action? What should we be willing to do?

These were the questions we confronted when we started our journey to improve healthcare communication. Our culture prioritized excellence in medical and surgical care above all other goals, an academic medical center in which being an excellent clinician was a more prominent priority than publishing research or bringing in grant dollars. So why weren't our patients reporting that they felt that they were the center of our attention?

The issues we confronted are common across American healthcare institutions. While the challenge of communication in healthcare has often been dumbed down to something along the lines of "doctors are poor communicators," that rang false to us. When we looked at our colleagues, we saw amazingly talented people who were deeply committed to the care of their patients. The time and effort they expended, striving to make the right medical decisions for their patients, was inspiring. And their ability to articulate how they thought and the basis of their decisions contradicted any notion that they couldn't communicate clearly. We noted that when we looked outside of medicine, we saw the same problems in communication that people often complain about in healthcare. Communicating and forming relationships with other human beings is one of the great challenges we face in life and, for the most part, we are expected to figure this out on our own through a process of trial and error. We often communicate poorly in our marriages, with our children or parents, in our work, and even with ourselves.

What sets healthcare apart is that it is a world of particularly difficult conversations and stressful relationships. Patients are sick, treatments are often less than fully effective, and complex medical information must be translated into a form comprehensible to laypersons. If you pulled a stranger off the streets and asked her to sit down with someone that she has never met and tell him that he had a terminal illness or that one of his loved ones had died or that the medical field had not figured out how to make his chronic pain go away, she would refuse and run. These are difficult conversations, and the intensity of training in our experience must be commensurate with the difficulty.

Moreover, illness transports many of us to a strongly emotional state, while clinicians are generally more comfortable in the cognitive realm. Plato described this as a chariot with two winged horses to represent the soul trying to direct rational and irrational pulls. A theme in many observational studies of physicians in practice is the strong tendency to respond to patient emotion with cognitive reasoning. Although we like to think that our rationality can tame emotions, we humans are much more prone to letting our emotions take over our rationality. We decide to eat the cake when we feel sad, even though we know it's not great for our health. We delay making the colonoscopy appointment because we are anxious about the procedure, but we know finding cancer is important. When we feel emotional distress, our rational brain contrives actions that will diminish our distress. But it is our distress that governs our behavior.

Physicians will avoid having tough conversations or resort to labeling patients as a means of coping with the stress of actually communicating with them. We walk into a room and see "the pain patient" demanding narcotics. We don't have the power to eliminate the pain. We are confronted with our helplessness to fix the patient's problem, while at the same time we resent the pressure from the patient to prescribe a medication that we think will do more harm than good. We see a middle-aged mother or father of young children who is diagnosed with a terminal illness and desperately wants more time alive than we have the power to give. We have parents who are convinced that antibiotics will cure their child's viral upper respiratory tract infection despite all the evidence to the contrary. What words make sense, and when did we learn them? How long is it fair to make our other patients wait while we "try our best" with the person in front of us?

And will our department administrator yell at us for taking too much time with these patients and not clocking enough Relative Value Units (RVUs)?

What we came to realize was that clinicians had generally not been provided with an opportunity to study and practice healthcare communication skills the way they had been required to study and practice medical decision making, the maneuvers of the physical examination, and invasive medical procedures. In many ways, communication skills are similar to physical examination skills. They need to be practiced, like motor skills, and skilled feedback must be provided so that practitioners can learn from their past performance.

Most important, we came to appreciate that relationships lay at the center of healthcare. All work was conducted in the context of relationships: clinician-patient, doctor-doctor, nurse-doctor, attending-resident, clinician–family member, and so on. Human beings feel a need to be seen and heard, to feel a sense of belonging and connection, to be appreciated. If we ignore those needs and focus only on physiological and cognitive processes, we alienate patients and make them feel that they and their experiences are invisible to us.

Our project became an effort to build connections, nurture relationship skills, and awaken our and our colleagues' latent empathic capacities so that not only our patients, but also we clinicians would feel a greater sense of belonging and appreciation. Practicing relationship-centered communication skills turned out to be a highly effective way of reengaging clinicians with why they pursued healthcare careers in the first place. It reminded them of what made the work rewarding and fulfilling. After all, at the end of the day, the patient is much more interesting than the disease.

Equally important, we aimed to model the behaviors that we thought would help them in their work with patients. If we wanted them to listen to their patients, then we needed to listen to them. If we wanted them to express empathy with their patients, then we needed to express empathy with them. If we wanted them to work in a collaborative way with patients, then we needed to work in a collaborative way with them. Lecturing physicians not to lecture patients is hypocritical. So, too, is telling clinicians to just deal with it when they are struggling to adjust to the new reality of ubiquitous patient satisfaction surveys. If we collectively can move healthcare institutions to work from top to bottom in a more relationship-centered way, we will accomplish a profound and valuable change of culture that will help patients and healthcare workers alike.

These issues led us to reject the model of patient-centered communication and instead to focus on relationship-centered communication. We did not want to tell clinicians that they were in the periphery while the patient was in the center. Rather, we wanted to challenge them to develop skills that would help them establish more effective, functional, and satisfying relationships with patients, relationships in which both the patient's and the clinician's experience mattered. We believe that relationships are therapeutic and that relationships function best when all parties to the relationship matter.

Calling Ms. Hide "annoying," "crazy," or "manipulative" is easy, expected, basic even. What requires actual skill is to move beyond these labels and find Ms. Hide. For Ms. Hide, there is no lurking, hidden medical diagnosis that no one has discovered yet after months of testing. For this individual, that isn't the medical challenge to be solved. But there is a young woman with unimaginable wounds dating from her teenage years that haven't healed and that keep asking to be seen. Maybe, just maybe, the most therapeutic thing we can ever do is to look for her in all of our patients.

Acknowledgments

This isn't Adrienne and Tim's book; it's our team's book. So, first and foremost, we want to thank our team:

Katie Neuendorf, the director of our Center of Excellence in Healthcare Communication (CEHC). She is a visionary. We have never met a more talented communication facilitator. She held steadfastly to the idea that one of the most important things to do is to tell people like it is. To AB, she has been a friend and a colleague that I am honored to know.

Amy Windover. We had grandiose ideas about how to go about working with communication skills in experienced clinicians, and Amy grounded us in competencies and intelligent design. Although she has a knack for creating beautiful and meaningful curricula, she has also been a driving force and dear friend.

Jessica Crow, our project manager who has been with us since the beginning. She makes better lists than anyone we know and keeps us all on task. More than that, she has kept it real and honest in tough times and has been loyal to the end.

Lacey Kay. She will probably be embarrassed that her name is even on this list and prefers to work behind the scenes, but we all know that we would be lost without her.

Our facilitator team. We could list all of you, but it would make more sense to spend the space talking about you. An unprecedented team of advanced care providers, surgeons, and medicine specialists. You all rallied around the concept of a realistic program founded in relationships, and the family we created surpassed all expectations. We are absolutely humbled by all of you.

We have been able to develop this work creatively and in an evidence-based fashion because of wonderful mentors and partners: Dr. Tony Back has led communication skills courses for years and was generous in sharing his experience and insight. Dr. Walter Baile, who has been one of the great mentors of TG's career and a dear confidant to AB. Rebecca Walters brings value and compassion to the powerful work she does and touched us with her work. We also want to recognize the American Academy on Communication in Healthcare, an organization that encouraged us about the possibilities, including the notion of consistently treating each other with appreciation and empathy. Dr. Calvin Chou has been an amazing colleague and friend to us both.

Last, we want to thank our patients. It is a deep privilege to be invited into your lives. We have learned immensely about humanity and about life and death and love and meaning from you. At the most fundamental level, our work on communication is about you.

AB Acknowledgments

Rich Frankel. From the moment we met, I knew I had a kindred spirit and soul in you. Your mentorship has expanded well beyond a book or the work into a friendship that I will forever cherish. My goal, however, is to write a paper on something about which you haven't already written.

Jim Merlino. You barreled down a path that no one had ever been down, and you encouraged me to do the same. The program flourished under your watch, and we accomplished what we did because you broke down all the barriers. For all your guts and titles, my favorite is simply friend.

Kelly Hancock. A dear friend and trusted partner. You have an eye for reality, a touching humility, and a passion for the front line—it's a powerful combination for someone in your role as chief nursing officer. Thank you for the vents and peps and nudges and unwavering support.

Toby Cosgrove. In our one-on-one meetings, I developed a new appreciation for your commitment to Patients First. It's not a tagline or fad for you—it is woven into your fabric. You articulate it at every turn and in your decisions for the organization. You supported communication skills training from the very beginning, spoke to the work on the world stage, and shared your own stories with our team. You told me once not to worry about nonsense and to drive the work, which is exactly what you've inspired me to do.

Linda McHugh. The best thing about my office was that it was right next to yours. I continue to be humbled by your candor, guidance, and enthusiasm for doing the right thing for people. And . . . the fastest book reader I ever met.

Michael Modic. When I first met you, we spoke about the meaning of this work, and you supported me before I even knew what I was doing. In the most interesting moments in my career and life, you have struck me with your leadership and insight. I owe so much to you.

Dan Bokar. A data genius and friend who brings humanism to the numbers and is deeply connected to the work in a way that inspires everyone around you, including me.

Carmen Kestranek. Your leadership and humility make the work fun, and your friendship is invaluable. At times, it was just you and me and . . . we made it through.

Office of Patient Experience team. Thanks for believing.

Kathy Carrick. My partner in crime and executive assistant. Without you, nothing is possible.

My mom, Regina. There are no words to thank you that would do you justice. You have survived more than most and taught me so much about resilience, as well as the need for play and laughter. You have witnessed my darkest moments and walked with me through them.

My brother, Alan. Thank you for the life lessons and love, especially the ones where you rightly told me, "What you're doing isn't working." My stepfather, John, for always supporting me.

To my family, Peter, Grant, and Grayson, for infusing my days with craziness and love and snuggles. Your patience for these long nights spent writing is forever appreciated.

To my dear friends. You've seen me through it all. I thank you.

TG Acknowledgments

There are so many people to whom I owe thanks for enabling my work on communication skills training. Even before heading to medical school, my teachers and professors in English literature, particularly Charles Chatfield and Phil Weinstein, trained me to listen carefully and to consider the impact of words and phrases. The Columbia University School of Journalism taught me to think seriously about how hard it can be to convey complex information accurately to those who have low or intermediate literacy.

My career would have been much less successful without the strong early support of my medical school mentor, Dr. Tom Raffin, who took me under his wing and drew me a map. In residency, Dr. Marshall Wolf showed so much faith in me that I could only go along as if I believed in myself. More important, he modeled for me the kind of doctor I aspired to be. At Dana-Farber Cancer Institute, Phil Kantoff gave me the freedom and support to figure out what I wanted to do and to start doing it. As with Dr. Raffin, I'm not sure where I would be without his key early investment in my career.

I want to thank my institute and department chairs who have supported me and given me time for this work: Dr. Derek Raghavan, Dr. Brian Bolwell, Dr. Robert Dreicer, and Dr. Matt Kalaycio, as well as Dr. Jim Merlino and Dr. Adrienne Boissy. In the communication realm, I am in debt to early mentors: Dr. Raffin taught me about bioethics and doctor-patient communication. At Dana-Farber Cancer Institute, Dr. Susan Block encouraged me to take my interest in healthcare communication seriously, provided sage advice, and led me to Tony Back. I have been blessed to have as my partner in this work for the past seven years Dr. Adrienne Boissy. Her passion and the clarity of her vision have blazed our trail, and her friendship has made it much more fun.

Dr. Mikkael Sekeres has been a strong and loyal friend who has continuously encouraged me in my work on communication skills and has graciously edited essays I have written and inspired me with his own writing.

My parents have encouraged me with love and resources from the day I was born, and there is no way to put into words what I owe them. I'm hoping to pay it forward. My children, Maxine and Joseph, and my wife, Heather, have been extremely patient as I have spent nights and weekends and holidays working on communication skills projects and writing and editing this book. I am hugely grateful for their patience and their love. You three give my life its meaning.

"I Already Know This" and "Patients Know I Care"

Designing a Culture That Is Ready for Communication Skills Training

"Do you teach empathy at Cleveland Clinic?"

These words would forever change our organization. It was 2006 and our CEO, Dr. Toby Cosgrove, had been invited to speak at Harvard Business School. As he finished his comments, a young student named Kara Medoff Barnett raised her hand. She spoke of her father, a physician, who needed a mitral valve surgery and how their family decided where to have his heart surgery done. They were familiar with the excellent cardiac outcomes we had, yet

1

ultimately they decided against Cleveland Clinic for his care "because we heard you had no empathy."

Reflecting on this experience, Cosgrove was "floored."[1] Ten days later, he was in Saudi Arabia attending the dedication of an International Medical City. As he listened to the president of the hospital speak about the type of care they were hoping to provide, he looked over at the king and saw that he was crying. As he looked out into the audience, he realized they were crying, too. In that moment, he recognized, "We are really missing something. We need to treat the soul and spirit of the patient, not just the body."

Patients First

One of the most important changes was Cosgrove's conception of Patients First as Cleveland Clinic's motto. Patients First became the True North of the organization. What this meant on the ground level was that any strategic decisions or initiatives that the organization put forward had to involve improving the care and experience of our patients at their core. Although there was marketing associated with the Patients First model and many caregivers were skeptical, repeated messaging reinforced that we all exist for the care of the patient. When there was pushback about the motto, it was usually in the form of "patients first and caregivers last." That was a noteworthy reflection of our culture at the time. As an organization, we know that both patients and caregivers are important and have intrinsic value. If Patients First was really going to permeate our culture, we would need to be intentional about building programs that had perceived value to the caregivers we wanted to reach. Thinking about how we could evolve programs that not only enhanced the patient experience, but also the experience of our caregivers remains a critical, foundational approach.

Many changes occurred during these years that helped to evolve our culture toward a more patient-centered environment. Cosgrove wanted to align care physically around the patient. He wanted to streamline service lines so that cardiothoracic surgeons worked alongside cardiologists and radiologists to deliver exceptional cardiac care, to break down the silos of a traditional academic structure, and to create teams of diverse individuals and professionals all working toward Patients First. Although there was initial concern about what that would feel like or look like, he was effective in messaging that alignment was simply the right thing to do for patients. This purpose resonated with most of our caregivers.

Another change that reinforced the Patients First principle was instituting same-day appointments. Although there are certainly business cases for creating same-day access, it was an organizational initiative that put the needs of the patient front and center. The move required a radical shift in the way scheduling had always been done. Cosgrove was unwavering in the idea that same-day access had to occur; however, he deferred to individual institutes as to how that would be executed. The idea was simple. If people can't access your services, it doesn't really matter how wonderful they are. Patients want to be seen.

We also created Voice of the Patient Advisory Councils (VPACs) throughout the healthcare system. They gave us input on policies regarding conflicts of interest and disruptive physicians, and feedback on facilities. On one occasion, a VPAC asked that members of an architectural firm that was presenting plans on a new building spend a day in a wheelchair and report back to them. The council input was especially relevant because the plans were for a new Neurological Institute. Even parking services were altered to allow patients access to the first few floors of a garage, and physician and employee parking was moved more distally.

Recognizing the healing power of art in the environment on individual patients, we established an Arts & Medicine Institute. At times, our caregivers play the piano and our patients perform, all with the goal of cultivating an environment of healing. Cosgrove's commitment to patient experience and to easing the anxiety and fears of patients also bore itself out in the environmental design. When entertaining ideas for a new water display to mark the entrance to Cleveland Clinic, a design firm pitched an idea for an intricate, complex, and light-enhanced feature. Cosgrove challenged the designers: "Do you know what our patients are feeling when they walk through these doors? They are afraid and scared. It's our job to create a sense of calm, and the most calming thing I can think of is a smooth body of water." And that's what we got. A simple, round water feature with infinity edges and subtle lighting.

Patients First was here to stay.

Chief Experience Officer

In 2008 Cosgrove created the executive position of chief experience officer (CXO) after reading an article about the impact a CXO could have on integrating patient experience and organizational priority.[2] He hired Dr. Bridget Duffy, a dermatologist by training, who led the Office of Patient Experience. Her passion for patient experience was palpable and highlighted the experiences of both our patients and caregivers to the highest levels of the organization. She was exceptionally effective at sharing the stories of our patients and inspiring many of us to want to be better at what we did.

In 2009 Dr. Jim Merlino became the CXO. A colorectal surgeon by training, the most powerfully effective quality Merlino had was his ability to speak of his personal experience and leverage it for organizational culture change. He told the story of his father, who had been admitted to Cleveland Clinic for what was supposed to be a routine biopsy. But after several days of complications, his father arrested and died. Merlino described the agony of having to witness his father being reduced to "his most vulnerable state" and the pain of his actual loss. Merlino's story moved all who heard it, and he performed his role with a very personal passion for the work.[3] Under his leadership, the Office of Patient Experience thrived (Figure 1.1), and Cleveland Clinic moved up from the 8th percentile in patient satisfaction to about the 70th.

FIGURE 1.1 **Organizational Structure of the Office of Patient Experience**

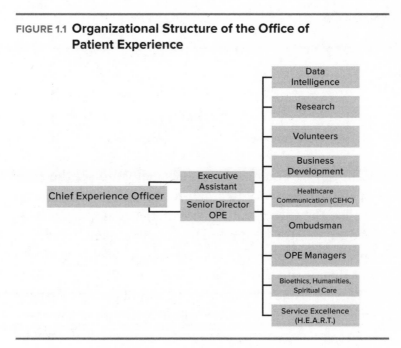

Merlino partnered with Kelly Hancock, our chief nursing officer, who lives and breathes this work, to drive experience efforts across the system. We defined Patients First as safe care, high-quality care, in the context of patient satisfaction, and value. This was a critical step in our journey. What's powerful about this definition is that patient experience isn't merely an average of patient satisfaction scores. Just as caregiver experience isn't simply an average of their engagement scores. With the Centers for Medicaid and Medicare Services (CMS) reserving the right to change patient satisfaction questions or metrics at any time, designing a patient experience strategy simply to improve your Hospital Consumer Assessment of Healthcare Providers and Systems (HCAHPS) scores is chasing a number and not evolving a culture. Patient experience cannot exist irrespective of teamwork, excellent clinical care, and superior outcomes. We wanted a culture of patient experience.

> *Without a definition of patient experience, it is very difficult to improve it.*

The Clinic organized a massive effort to set the stage for patient experience in a half-day program that came to be called the Cleveland Clinic Experience (CCE). In these sessions, healthcare providers, environmental services employees, and administrators sat around a table with a single facilitator and a learning map (Figure 1.2).

We spent time talking about the why of Patients First, the values of the organization, our role in patient experience, and learned service recovery skills in a program called Respond with H.E.A.R.T.™ Within these sessions, the term *caregiver* was introduced and equalized the playing field by breaking down barriers between traditional staff, faculty, and employees. We *all* became caregivers. All 43,000 Cleveland Clinic caregivers completed the training in a year and a half.

FIGURE 1.2 The Cleveland Clinic Experience Learning Map

Service Recovery at Cleveland Clinic: Respond with H.E.A.R.T.

Hear the story
  Listen attentively.

Empathize
  "I can see/hear that you are upset."

Apologize
  "I'm sorry you were disappointed."

Respond to the problem
  "What can I do to help?"

Thank them
  "Thank you for taking the time to tell me about this."

Simply changing the term was not enough. Occasionally during CCE, physicians leaned back in their chairs away from the table. They were there, but they weren't. Many of these participants received letters from the chief of staff about needing to reattend the course after leaving early or not participating in the process with everyone else. Many clinicians felt these sessions were of variable value to them, yet what they failed to appreciate was the impact of their presence and, in particular, their disengagement. If clinicians at a physician-led organization show up for an educational program or activity, this carries the message to others that the effort has value and is a priority for the organization. If they show up, lean back in their chairs, and leave early, then they give the message that as physician leaders at this organization, we don't really have to participate like everyone else. There seemed to be a lack of self-awareness that as a physician, you are a leader, and your behavior is watched and interpreted. Modeling that patient experience matters to all of us—or it doesn't—is a choice we all make and for which we would be held accountable.

Cleveland Clinic also produced an "empathy video," which was a window into the lives of patients and caregivers.[4] Currently, it has more than 2 million views on YouTube. I became aware of the video's impact when I went to speak at a national patient experience summit and was prepared to show it as part of my presentation. To my surprise, the speaker right before me from a Texas healthcare system played it. When we've asked people what is so powerful about this video, the answers are reminders of why we are here. The video honors that each of us has a story that we carry with us into every interaction. This video embodied the cultural transformation that was taking place at Cleveland Clinic at the time.

> *If you knew their story, you probably would treat them differently.*

The Physician

The road to becoming a physician isn't easy. We start with the purpose of wanting to help others, then our empathy erodes throughout residency once we become exposed to the "real" world of medicine and hidden curricula of training.[5] The ability to empathize never recovers to what it originally was. If we step back and think about this for a minute with an open mind, is it really a reasonable expectation that we will produce empathic caregivers when we don't treat caregivers with respect and empathy during their training? There are extremes of disruptive behavior and famous stories of doctors throwing tantrums or surgical instruments, but there are also some significant offensive generalizations about physicians.

We sat in a national meeting recently where the presenters proposed that the only way to incentivize physicians was to give them bonuses. Yet the stark reality of the profession is that many physicians no longer find joy in their work. Physicians remain in the highest risk group for professions committing suicide, and over half of them are burned out. Thinking of them as a group that, at times, may be suffering just as much as patients is essential to also seeing them as human.

The World

The world of healthcare is changing. In 2001, the Institute of Medicine published *Crossing the Quality Chasm*, a report that called for patient-centered care.[6] It identified key principles to redefine healthcare that included attending to patients' values and beliefs, recognizing the value of healing relationships and shared decision making, the need to communicate effectively, and customizing care to the patient. The Patient Protection and Affordable Care Act (H.R.3590) and the Health Care Education and Reconciliation Act (H.R.4872) are together known as the Affordable Care Act (ACA). What the ACA outlines is that the old fee-for-service model in healthcare will be replaced by a value-based purchasing model. The Centers for Medicare and Medicaid were driving the point that healthcare institutions were accountable for cost, health outcomes, and experience, the so-called Triple Aim.[7] Included in these changes is tying reimbursement to hospital performance in four areas: quality and safety, patient experience, value, and outcomes. Over time, the schedule for the percentage of Medicare reimbursements dependent upon these metrics will increase every year, and the percentage of each category will also change.

Not only are hospitals accountable, so are individual clinicians according to certain metrics. Patient satisfaction surveys cover multiple domains of care, including communication, discharge, pain management, responsiveness, accessibility, and so on. How did doctors communicate? Did they spend enough time with you? Did you feel as though you were part of the decision making? And on the inpatient side, did you perceive that the healthcare team worked well together? Were your medications explained to you? Did the nurses communicate? There is increasing pressure on individual care providers to evaluate critically the way we practice. This may feel uncomfortable for clinicians, given that formerly we typically had free rein to provide care we felt was appropriate, regardless of cost or evidence. In fact, most of us went into healthcare so that we could function independently, provide great care to patients, enjoy financial security, and exercise control over the way we practice. The very idea that CMS or the hospital is now looking over our shoulders and infiltrating our management is difficult, understandably so. The reality is that "change is inevitable, growth is optional."

As daunting as all these changes are to the individual clinician, they provide the burning platform that is critical to creating real change. Simply put, the way we had always done it wasn't going to work anymore.

Transparency

Cosgrove was innovative in thinking about how transparency would drive behavior. He knew that when heart surgical outcomes were published, quality improved. He articulated a desire to have patient experience metrics available to individual physicians. Currently, these scores are available on Physician Compare offered through Medicare. In addition, hospital systems, including Cleveland Clinic, have posted their patient feedback as captured in patient satisfaction surveys to the public on their websites. Multiple websites, including Healthgrades and Vitals, do this as well, but the problem is that there is no confirmation that the reviewer ever saw a given clinician, reviews can exist based on only one or two surveys, and people can say just about anything. Yet, with roughly 60 percent of patients looking for physicians online, transparency is not going away.[8]

As highlighted by Merlino, 72 percent of negative HCAHPS comments were about communication (respect, compassion, listening, who is in charge, and the plan). We knew that no single score is enough to build a story of a given provider's ability to communicate, but several scores pulled from different data sets can.

In 2010–2011, Cleveland Clinic rolled out individual clinician reporting of inpatient and outpatient communication scores. There was fear that this would cause a major uprising. For about six months, we blinded the scores so that physicians knew how their own scores compared with others in their department, but their colleagues' scores were not identified by name. We didn't hear a peep. Now, however, all clinicians can see each other's performance on inpatient and outpatient communication domains from HCAHPS, Clinical Group Consumer Assessment of Healthcare Providers and Systems (CGCAHPS), and patient complaints. For a competitive population, transparency can change behavior. No clinician likes to see his or her name on the bottom of any performance list. However, many cannot improve their communication scores simply by trying. They don't always know what to do or say differently. They may not even be aware of what their current practice is. Showing physicians where they are not meeting a target and then not offering any solutions to help them achieve the target is counterproductive and may result in further disengagement. Transparency can raise awareness of behavior, but to fully support our staff, we needed to offer the appropriate training. The stage was set for communication skills programs.

Strategy and Myth

Despite all the efforts made to drive Patients First, we still needed a strategy to engage physicians. Although the government had built a burning platform, physicians still struggled to see which pieces we could influence. Certainly, we could improve safety and quality, and we also control how we communicate, which is core to the patient experience. Not only does how well caregivers communicate drive overall patient satisfaction ratings, it also drives safety and quality and lowers the risk of being sued for malpractice.

We spent over a year developing our content and a year piloting it, a process we detail in this book. One thing we learned, however, is that no matter how strong your content or how powerful your curriculum, significant vision and strategy is vital to bringing clinicians to the course itself. In fact, when we talk about the communication program nationally, people rarely ask about the content—they are most curious about how to get clinicians engaged. This brings up several important arguments we've heard about why communication skills aren't important or why training won't work and how you might respond to them (Table 1.1).

1. Physicians don't care

By and large, this is simply not true. In our experience, the perception of apathetic physicians is much more likely a product of today's healthcare environment. At times, we have all struggled with the sheer volume of information and tasks coming at us: electronic medical record messages, prescription refills, MyChart messages, alerts about open encounters, forms that need signing, physician metrics to document and complete, consent forms, e-mail messages, and our pagers, among many others. We must recognize that as we improve our electronic documentation, we seem to get better at

---

TABLE 1.1 **Exploding Myths**

*Five Myths about Communication
Training and Approaches for Discussion*

Myth: Physicians don't care.
• Acknowledge and listen to stress factors and causes of burnout.
• Ask physicians about what gives their work meaning—usually it's time with patients.
• Discover what the physician *does* care about, and build from that.

Myth: Basic communication skills aren't needed.
• Explore real-world personal and professional challenges caused by basic skill deficits.
• Elicit the physicians' own stories—the cases that haunt them.
• Link basic skills to leadership development.
• Promote lifelong learning and sharing of best practices for a given scenario or population.

Myth: You can't teach empathy.
• Know and share the decades of evidence that you can.
• Stay curious about prior learning experiences with empathy and communication.
• Demonstrate that empathic behaviors can be taught through innovative design.

Myth: Residents, not staff, need the training.
• Learning is lifelong for staff and trainees.
• Residents watch staff closely and learn from their behaviors, including communication skills.
• By dedicating attention to communication skills, staff attendings message its importance and value.
• Caring for patients is a team sport, so everyone has a responsibility.

Myth: Communication training is all about HCAHPS scores.
• Acknowledge that changes in healthcare are difficult.
• Expand the discussion to how communication skills training benefits the individual clinician.
• Show how effective communication impacts outcomes, satisfaction, safety, and efficiency.

---

generating it. Multiple studies have demonstrated physician dissatisfaction with feeling pulled away from our patients. That's just our experience. If you are a community physician who rounds alone in the hospital before starting your own clinic, you may go back to the hospital at the end of the day and still have to finish your notes. We must appreciate that many of our providers are overwhelmed, disconnected, and unhappy about it. Expecting our community to simply sign up for a good course is wishful thinking. Physicians are making choices about their time, and communication courses fall low on the list of priorities. In designing and executing communication courses, we must acknowledge and address these physician concerns head on.

2. Doctors don't need foundational communication skills

The irony of communication skills programs is that many among the target audience don't think they need them. We've heard repeatedly, "I'm very good at this. I've been in practice a long time," "You don't really value communication. This is about the scores," "If I just gave more narcotics, my scores would be better," "My patients really like me," or "So you want me to be soft and fluffy instead of doing my job?" As one participant put it, "I thought—being an empathic sort and thorough in history taking for over 25 years—I would have little to learn." To be honest, we were a bit surprised by our fellow physicians' lack of willingness to embrace foundational communication skills and the failure to recognize that if we are not willing to learn and practice relationship-centered communication skills, how can we be sure our patients are benefiting from them? Our students? Many told us that they studied communication skills in medical school, and then the skills were effectively squashed out during training. Then we unleash them as staff physicians and never provide them with any feedback on their communication skills, despite giving them ultimate responsibility for a patient's clinical care and experience. We then promote our caregivers into leadership positions where they have challenging management conversations without training or preparation. If we do not open ourselves to the process of enhancing our skill sets, our performance will peak and remain stagnant. How can we as a healthcare community promote lifelong learning when we resist learning ourselves? Why is it that we believe that completing our fellowship means we have learned all there is to learn? In other fields, the idea that you already know everything you need to know is not an accepted norm, and yet in medicine it is.[9] Why does Serena Williams have a tennis coach? Doesn't she know what she is doing by now?

3. Physicians can't be taught to be empathic— you have it or you don't

There's been about 30 years of research in the field of communication skills training and its impact on the individual clinician. Multiple meta-analyses have been completed. Through the work of Wendy Levinson and others, we know that effective communication impacts malpractice claims. We know that it also impacts patient safety and quality, physician experience, patient experience, and there is an emerging body of literature on its impact on health outcomes.[10]

We are hardwired for empathy, and the concept matures with the growing brain. Functional MRI studies have expanded our understanding.[11] Although a personality and habits may be firmly rooted, the use and acquisition of new relationship-centered communication skills is a choice, as is any meaningful behavior change. In our experience, physicians must be receptive to learning new things and then choose to do a few things differently in order for communication skills training to have an impact. By simply saying it is an innate skill, clinicians excuse themselves from having to acquire and master it.

Rather than create a checklist of all communication skills that a clinician should learn, we promote the concept of reflective competence. With respect to communication skills, this is the ability to reflect on the words that come out of our mouths, get feedback on them, and then practice new language deliberately and intentionally.

4. The residents (or consultants) need this training more than I do

Today, more than ever, we are providing care in teams. Sometimes hospital patients see a single clinician; other times, they see a rotating, dynamic team. From our standpoint, this simply raises the bar. If your score is reliant on 30 other people, then you should be working hard to get those 30 other people on the same page. When we have the option of who to choose for a consult, we should exercise that option. If we don't, we should communicate directly with patients that as the attending staff in charge, all final decisions regarding their care will be the result of a discussion of the issue between us and them.

Residents are watching the staff. It's how they learn the art of medicine. If the staff don't model these skills, or can't identify what they are or why they were used, the team won't learn them. This latter part is critical. On multiple occasions, I've been told that Dr. X is really well liked by patients. "What does he say or do that makes him effective?" we would ask. "What do you mean?" is usually the response. If we push harder and ask for specific words or phrases that resonated with the patient, we sometimes hear, "He really listened" or "He sat down." What is fascinating about these exchanges is that if *we* cannot identify effective language that has the most impact on our patients, we lose the opportunity to teach it to others. Oftentimes, effective practitioners are simply identified as "nice" or "friendly." This undermines the complexity and intricacy of effective communication. A doctor can be nice without using reflective listening, the skill of reflecting back to the patient the content or emotion of what was just said to reinforce that it was heard. He can be nice without empathizing. She can be friendly without shared decision making. Our goal is not simply to be nice; we aim to form strong, authentic, caring, and mutually respectful relationships with effective skills.

If there are multiple people on your team, as there often are, then many of the medical details are already known. You may even have heard them before you walk into the room. If that's the case, then you have the luxury of being able to fully engage with the person. The patient is already known.[12] The human being is not.

5. This is just about the scores

When we hear the comment "This is just about the scores" during the communication course, we typically respond, "Of course we live in a new healthcare environment. We all recognize that. However, for me as your colleague, this work means much more and has transformed my practice. I keep doing it so that I can inspire the same in my colleagues."

We rolled out our Foundations of Healthcare Communication course (FHC) shortly after the communication scores became transparent. As an institution, Cleveland Clinic wanted to hold people accountable for their scores, while also providing them with the educational resources to improve and developing communication skills training that took into account how difficult it is to be an effective communicator in today's practice.

> Although the origins predate the current emphasis on HCAHPS scores, the course contents could not have been more timely. I am going to try some of the techniques that I learned tomorrow. I really appreciate your willingness to do this. I imagine that it is not easy to deal with a bunch of doctors.
>
> —COURSE PARTICIPANT

Caregivers are having high-stakes conversations with patients and families daily without any feedback about how to do it or what might be more effective next time. This goes beyond service excellence or customer service. Some doctors are very frustrated by challenging conversations with patients for which they don't feel well prepared. If the conversation doesn't go well, there is an emotional impact on the provider that increases his or her sense of helplessness. In addition, we know that communication gaps are at the root of ethics consultations,[13] calls to the ombudsman's office, and safety issues. As an organization committed to the success of our caregivers and the care of our patients, Cleveland Clinic provided the skills and tools our people need.

Fueled by a changing healthcare landscape that is driving transparency and individual physician accountability, the burning platform for communication skills training across the health system was created. Because we began our journey developing a communication skills program for physicians, we will focus on them. We know full well that all caregivers impact the patient experience, and we also know that many clinicians have unique communication needs given the complexity of their work. We've included the perspectives of advanced care providers to date and have much more to learn about this group, as well as nursing. We've grown and expanded since then, but this is the story of the beginning of a lifelong journey.

The answer is yes, we teach empathy at Cleveland Clinic.

Chapter 2

Leveraging Your Burning Platform

Our Story

My invitation to develop a communication skills program for Cleveland Clinic was entirely unglamorous. Merlino took me for coffee and, as we were catching up, asked if I would take on such a role. Without thinking, I said, "Yes." As I (Adrienne Boissy) walked out of that meeting, I had the distinct feeling that I had accepted an enormous job that I felt unqualified to do. I'm a neurologist, not an educator or communications guru. By the time I made it back to my own office, I had started wondering about my colleagues and friends. How would I ever be able to deliver something to them that would matter? By the time I made it home, I had successfully talked myself out of the job. No way could we engage seasoned clinicians in communication skills training. But as I considered how I would want to learn communication skills, I decided that this was the kind of chance I needed to grab and run with. When was the last time someone helped me understand how to have the tough conversations? What if we could actually build something that would help all of us feel more comfortable having the difficult talks? The challenge was enticing. To his credit, Merlino gave me a blank slate to work on and told me to figure it out. So off I went.

Caregivers in healthcare are compassionate, dedicated, and hardworking. Physicians are also data-driven, outcome-focused, and default thinkers. When we tell patients we teach communication skills to physicians, they say, "Thank goodness!" When we tell educators, they say, "Good luck!" And when we tell physicians, they typically say, "What for?" When I was swapping ideas one day with Ananth Raman from Harvard Business School, he highlighted that we might learn something from the seat belt industry. How do you convince people that they need something they don't think they need?

Task Force Assembly

The path was totally uncertain, so it seemed best to gather a team of like-minded believers in the concept of relationship-centered communication who could help define it. The core group included Dr. David Vogt (senior hepatobiliary surgeon), Dr. Amy Windover (psychologist and director of Cleveland Clinic Lerner College of Medicine communication skills training), Shirin Rastgoufard (project manager), Paula Timco (experience improvement), Dr. Tim Gilligan (oncologist), Dr. Vicente J. Velez (hospitalist), and me. We met monthly to survey the current institutional environment and to formulate an approach. What programs already existed and in what areas? Who led them, and what tools or models were they using? Areas we surveyed included the Office of Professional Learning and Development, Cleveland Clinic Lerner College of Medicine, Cleveland Clinic Academy (Education Institute), ACGME competencies, national communication organizations (American Academy of Communication in Healthcare [AACH], Institute for Healthcare Communication [IHC]), and comparable organizations. This inventory took a year. Yes, an entire year.

An important benefit to this approach was that we learned about what efforts were underway in our own house, which presented the opportunity to unite these efforts. This served us well. We learned that we were using outside consultants to teach communication skills, small departments were working with other institutions because they had previously worked there, and others had started their own programs for their own populations. After surveying what we had, we worked to unify the language and model we wanted to use. If you are hoping communication skills will stick, the effort can't be fragmented by diverse models taught throughout the organization. It has to be one unified program. We spent significant time learning about existing resources and rallying them.

Dr. Windover had a key role in leading communication skills training at the medical school, and she brought a depth of experience and credibility to the program. She was mapping to competencies and making sure we understood our objectives and built content to those. You'll notice that we didn't have a lot of faculty from the medical school initially, and as we look back on our ability to roll out a program that resonated with providers, this was a key—albeit accidental—decision. Because we didn't have a road map, we really were able to design a curriculum that was creative and adapted to our local culture. We were not a group of seasoned educators, and although we felt like fish out of water, we also felt unconstrained by philosophies of "that's the way it's done." At the same time, we were intentional about being guided by published evidence of what works.

We consulted with several groups in the initial evolution of the work. At the time, one of the most evidence-based models that existed was the Four Habit Model©, which had been created at Kaiser long before the patient satisfaction surveys of today. The habits are (1) creating rapport and collaboratively setting an agenda, (2) eliciting the patient perspective, (3) demonstrating empathy, and (4) delivering diagnostic information in a manner that the patient can understand. With gracious permission, we used this for our initial internal training for about a year before we developed our own for reasons that you will learn more about in Chapter 5. Several other models of communication exist. What is important to note about models is that they give providers a clear framework for approaching a given conversation rather than just seeing how it goes or winging it. When conversations are complex, emotions run high, and the risk of failure is great, why would we think that winging it is an effective strategy?

We worked and consulted with Dr. Walter Baile, Rebecca Walters, Dr. Tony Back, Dr. Calvin Chou, and the AACH at various points in our development. Each brought valuable tools to the table. Baile and Walters have unique methods of deepening the teaching of empathy through action, born out of psychodrama and sociodrama. Back and his organization, Vital Talk (previously OncoTalk) have been teaching palliative care discussions for years. AACH worked with us early on in small group facilitation methods. Chou, an internal medicine physician at the University of California, San Francisco (UCSF), was pivotal in our initial efforts to evolve a program. He helped us understand that communicating effectively is a discipline and inspired us all to drive it forward.

In working with these individuals, we recognized that strong content in the absence of a supportive culture is useless. You can build the best competency-based program with lists of references and train highly skilled facilitators, but if, at the end of the day, the chairs are empty, then the program has failed.

Here are some key first strategic steps that you might consider as you get started.

Initial Rollout, Recruitment, and Messaging

As Merlino highlighted in his book *Service Fanatics*, we knew our own data. Communication accounted for 72 percent of our negative patient comments and was one of the lowest performing HCAHPS measures. Cosgrove himself drove transparency of patient satisfaction communication scores across the organization. We built a profile of a given physician based on his or her inpatient, outpatient, and ombudsman's communication scores or issues (Table 2.1). This is critical to addressing some of the issues that clinicians raise about the scores. HCAHPS might not be a valid metric given its association with the discharging attending, but combining three sources of data for a given provider begins to build a story about how that provider communicates and is perceived by patients.

Transparency provides feedback to the individual provider, can fuel some healthy competition among clinicians who want to be the best at what they do, and generates some conversation among colleagues about what works and what doesn't. But simply measuring performance is not enough to achieve improvement: physicians need opportunities to learn and to practice new, more effective skills and to begin letting go of bad habits.

Calvin Chou trained an initial team of six clinicians: nephrologist Saul Nurko, cardiologist David Taylor, oncologist Tim Gilligan, hospitalist Vicente J. Velez, psychologist

TABLE 2.1 **Quarterly Individual Provider Reporting for Doctor Communication Across Data Sets**

Taussig Cancer Institute
Patient Experience Physician Report
(December 1, 2009 through November 30, 2010)

| HCAHPS | | Medical Practice | | | Ombudsman |
| | | | Domain | Recommend | Patients |
N	% Always	N	% V Good	% V Good	
25	77%	20	99%	100%	
29	63%	34	81%	81%	
		5	48%	40%	
		3	78%	100%	
14	71%	5	43%	40%	
23	86%	16	83%	84%	
		12	88%	82%	1
		2	100%	100%	
		29	87%	80%	
		11	73%	82%	
		5	68%	80%	1
8	71%	35	74%	83%	1
5	73%	14	87%	100%	
		5	68%	80%	1
8	71%	35	74%	83%	1
5	73%	14	87%	100%	

Amy Windover, and me. We *were* healthy skeptics. Chou was patient with all of our questions and moved us through the basics of facilitation. We developed a class using the Four Habit model as a foundation, with two facilitators for 8 to 12 participants.

Communication skills training is a tricky business. We were intentional about highlighting the benefits of the training for individual providers and asking for help rather than making it one more thing they had to do. When engaging healthy skeptics, we knew that messaging mattered. So we *invited* colleagues to attend. We asked them for their help in building a program that would depend on their feedback. And we meant it. Here is an excerpt of the initial invite:

> I am asking for your participation in one of the upcoming courses. Our goal is to build upon communication skills you already have and to collect feedback before the program is rolled out to all CCF staff. For others, your chairs or center directors have expressed support for the program and want their staff actively involved in this process.
>
> This is no small challenge given the time pressures we all face in clinical practice. The Office of Professional Staff Affairs supports your time away from patient care to participate in this process.

Once physicians attended (and they did), we asked them to recommend 10 of their colleagues, and the process repeated itself. Slowly, institute chairs began to reach out to us to train their physicians with the lowest HCAHPS communication scores. We nudged back, saying that the program leveraged the strength of everyone and wasn't designed to be punitive or to be a rehabilitation program. Ineffective communicators giving feedback to ineffective communicators would be . . . ineffective. We required the participation of both effective communicators and less effective communicators for our model to work. Institute chairs were receptive to this, and many committed their entire staff on the spot.

We invited like-minded peers to participate in the pilot phase to encourage attendance. This helped us learn how the course worked and how to improve it in the setting with interested participants who would be more forgiving of imperfections and more likely to recommend the course to others.

We quickly realized that talking about HCAHPS isn't very productive. We had included HCAHPS graphs in the slide deck, thinking that we would acknowledge the elephant in the room, and yet we found that invariably, the subsequent conversations drifted into "You are just doing this for HCAHPS" or "Just another flavor of the month." We received comments like these with empathy and listening, rather than defense of the program, and removed the slide. Regardless of the realities of the healthcare environment, for the facilitators of the course, this became a more personal movement to honor the complexities and intimacies of caregiving, therefore, HCAHPS didn't have a rightful place in that room.

We recognized early on that people may have assumptions about who trains in communications skills. You may have your own. We wanted to flip those assumptions on their head. Surgeons participated from the very beginning. I recruited them by making an appointment, introducing myself, explaining what we were doing, and asking them to sign up. One of them said with a smile, "I knew you would come for me one day."

Clinicians who were highly respected by their colleagues and had some organizational longevity (and were not already involved in any communication efforts) were also identified and invited.

This was a critical first step for us because there are many assumptions about the stereotypical surgeon and their communication style, just as there are assumptions about the type of person who may teach communication skills.

The night before we trained our first group of surgeons as facilitators, we had tremendous anxiety about whether they would take it seriously. But our fears were unfounded; they quickly embraced the training. "Just tell me the best thing to say, and I'll say it," they kept saying. They debated the evidence for the skills less and were diligent about getting the language we suggested right. One of the surgeon facilitators we trained was renowned clinically and yet not always for his interpersonal skills. To his absolute credit, he became passionate about learning more and enhancing his own skills. He offered to mentor some of our residents in their research in communication skills training. He wanted to meet after class to discuss and review his facilitation. This example is worth noting because during every class we heard a participant say, "Well, I heard Dr. X has undergone a transformation, so I wanted to learn more about this work. If he can change, I can, too." Never underestimate the power of one.

Regroup

After training 1,000 staff physicians over two years, we regrouped and redesigned the entire program into R.E.D.E. to Communicate™: Foundations of Healthcare Communication (FHC) (Table 2.2). We included competencies, checklists, pre- and postcourse evaluations, guides, and cue cards to make it clear to our facilitators and participants what was expected of them.

We realized that we wanted to own the training of our own facilitators. We designed a completely new Train the Trainer (TTT) model that built upon what we had learned, but now incorporated video with feedback, pairing to-be facilitators with more senior facilitators, creative moments that got people out of their chairs and interacting with each other, more opportunities for reflection, comprehensive evaluations, data collection processes, and narratives. We built a database of everyone who completed the training. Our TTT program runs for eight days (Table 2.3). Three days are spent showing what will be the final product, discussing evidence for communication skills training, explaining the educational theory behind it, and practicing. Then facilitators in training

TABLE 2.2 R.E.D.E. to Communicate: Foundations of Healthcare Communication Outline

1. Schedule:

8:00-9:30	Overview	12:30-1:15	Lunch
9:30-10:00	Phase I (didactic)	1:15-2:30	Phase III
10:00-10:15	Break	2:30-2:45	Break
10:15-11:15	Phase I (demo/skills practice)	2:45-4:00	Integrative Cases
11:15-12:30	Phase II	4:00-4:30	Wrap-up and evaluation

Facilitator	Time	Course Outline
	8:00–8:15 8:15–8:30	I. **Participant welcome and breakfast** II. **Administer pre-survey**
A	8:30–9:30	III. **Background and overview. Evidence for relationship-centered communication in healthcare.** **Defining the healthcare relationship and its benefits.** • Introductions • Reflective exercise • Warm ups with improv
B	9:30–11:15	IV. **R.E.D.E. Phase I: Establishing the relationship** • Brief, interactive didactic highlighting skills of conveying value and respect with welcome, collaboratively setting the agenda, use of the computer, and empathy with S.A.V.E. • Empathy video review and discussion • Empathy experiential exercise: Review several video clips for emotion recognition and brainstorm responses
	10:00–10:15	BREAK
	10:15–11:15	• Demonstration: Observe video or perform live demonstration of skills (inpatient and outpatient examples) • Skills Practice (50 min.): Break into two groups of six participants per facilitator and practice skills with rounds of feedback from peers, patient, and facilitators

A	11:15–12:30	**V. R.E.D.E. Phase II: Developing the relationship** • Brief interactive didactic highlighting skills of reflective listening, eliciting the patient narrative, and exploring patient perspective with V.I.E.W. • Reflective listening exercise • Demonstration: Observe video or perform live demonstration of skills (inpatient and outpatient examples) • Skills practice (50 min.): Break into two groups of six participants per facilitator and practice skills with rounds of feedback from peers, patient, and facilitators
	12:30–1:15	LUNCH
	1:15–1:20	CHECK-IN
B	1:20–2:30	**VI. R.E.D.E. Phase III: Engaging the relationship** • Brief, interactive didactic highlighting skills of sharing diagnosis and information, collaboratively developing treatment plan, providing closure, and dialoguing throughout with A.R.I.A. • Demonstration: Observe video or perform live demonstration of skills (inpatient and outpatient examples) • Skills practice (50 min.): Break into two groups of six participants per facilitator and practice skills with rounds of feedback from peers, patient, and facilitators
	2:30–2:45	BREAK/Planning
A	2:45–4:00	**VII. Integrative case(s):** participants pick scenarios • **Orient** Elicit actual challenging communication scenarios from participants and ask each participant to vote for their top three to determine one or two cases to practice • **Skills practice** As a larger group, role reversals, rolling skills practice, action methods, role interviewing, and improv will be employed as we work through challenging cases in a supportive setting • **Elicit** Feedback from (1) interviewer, (2) patient, (3) observers • **Summarize**
B	4:00–4:30	**VII. Wrap-up/Evaluation** • Thank you • Appreciative checkout • Behavioral commitment • Post course surveys

FIGURE 2.3 **R.E.D.E. to Communicate: Train the Trainer**

	Topics Covered	Location
Stage One (Days 1–3)	• Complete R.E.D.E. to Communicate: FHC • Evidence-based communication • Learning theory • Small group facilitation • Goal setting	Cleveland Clinic or locally
Stage Two (Days 4–6, two to four weeks later)	• Reflective practice • Presentation skills with video feedback • Co-facilitation • Integrative cases (improv and action methods) • Challenging scenarios in facilitation	Cleveland Clinic or locally
Stage Three (One Day) Co-facilitation	All of the above	Home institution
Stage Four (One Day) Observed facilitation	All of the above	Home institution

have a two- to four-week break. When we reassemble, we move on to videotaping presentation skills and giving feedback, more skills practice of how to run and orient learners to skills practice, and weaving in improv and action methods. One day is then spent at their home institution cofacilitating with them, and another day is spent watching them facilitate their own people with our feedback.

Within these Train the Trainer sessions, we foster relationships by having a cocktail hour so that newer facilitators can meet experienced facilitators and be welcomed into our facilitator family. We also have a congratulatory dinner for them at the end, and we present them with an inscribed gift based on what we have learned and admired about them during the training. During many of the sessions, we have an executive leader come to talk with them about how much leaders value this effort. Cosgrove came to one of these and told a powerful story about serving as a surgeon in Vietnam and not having much time to spend with hundreds of patients. He articulated that the one thing he did to let patients know that he was there was to touch them. He made a conscious effort "to touch a foot, a toe, a shoulder—anything" to let the person know he was connected to them. This was an unscripted and unplanned moment that made many of us personally believe that our CEO and organization supported the work we were being asked to do.

The second major change involved an advanced structure that fostered relationships among participants. We noted that many staff appreciated having an opportunity to come together and spend some time not just sharing communication challenges and tactics, but also engaging with each other. Given the size of our organization and the pressure we felt clinicians were under, we took notice. We also believe that there cannot be a meaningful patient experience without a meaningful clinician experience. Subsequently, building relationships among the team members became a strategic hidden curriculum for the program. In the new course we developed, informal and formal relationship-building opportunities were created, and the relationship-centered strategy became a parallel process—in other words, the facilitators were deliberate about forging relationships with participants at every moment. Key revisions included building in networking time at the beginning of the course and layering in more creative ways of building engagement.

Most important, it was at this point that we developed our own model of communication that is explored in Chapter 5. This was a critical step in our growth and expansion as a program. Dr. Windover initially presented this idea to me in 2013. I had asked her to collect the data and build a new program and model. When she first presented it, I wasn't so sure. Revise the course to emphasize first and foremost building relationships with patients? Did I even think about that in my own role? Yet as I reflected on it, I saw her brilliance.

A few years earlier, I had inherited a very large multiple sclerosis (MS) practice. I had no extra time with patients whom I was meeting for the first time, and I was intent on making sure I took good care of them. As I reviewed their records in advance, to my surprise, I found that some of the patients didn't actually have MS. That was odd. They had been coming to a MS center for years. At the same time, I realized that this wasn't a mistake or misdiagnosis. These were patients who had been labeled with MS for one reason or another, and yet we knew they didn't have it. I would later call this "therapeutic mislabeling."[1]

I would go into the examination room, introduce myself, and ask them about themselves: "Tell me something about yourself outside of your diagnosis." Then I would say, "Thanks for sharing a bit of yourself with me. So, I looked through all the records, and the great news is you don't have MS." What a relief. I had "fixed" their diagnosis and been honest about what they didn't have. I was stunned then when patients became angry and made comments like, "I'd like my old doctor back" or "If it's not MS, what is it?" or "I know that's what I have." What happened? I was honest, I gave accurate information, I asked them about themselves, and yet they were mad. Really? As Windover described why she was advocating for a relationship-centered approach, it hit me. Of course patients didn't hear what I was saying. I was giving what I thought was good news, which patients perceived as bad news and did so in the absence of a trusting relationship. It was an aha moment that would shape the rest of my career.

We rolled out our new R.E.D.E. to Communicate: FHC program in 2013, and shortly thereafter, we announced that completion of the course was "encouraged." That may be another word for "mandated" you might want to try. Persuading physicians to enroll was facilitated by the fact that our entire executive team completed the training and unblinded transparency had already been in place for several years at that point. As we worked with the executive team, we were struck by their own experiences as patients themselves or as caregivers to their loved ones. Training the executive team also bolstered the R.E.D.E. model because relationships are universal and the skills applied to our CFO and administrators as much as they did to clinicians. Relationship-centered communication skills are helpful in *all* human interactions.

We ramped up our ability to provide more frequent training as we were on an aggressive timeline. We were asked to train the entire attending staff population and all the residents in about seven months, an estimated 3,076 caregivers. We asked facilitators to teach three times a month, three times their original expected commitment. We needed to train more facilitators, for a critical mass of about 60. We mapped out each department and institute and sent them weekly reports on their registrations and completions of the course. When people said they couldn't or didn't want to complete the training, we responded with, "Thank you for sharing your thoughts. Dr. Cosgrove and our executive team have completed the training. Please consider attending so others may learn from you. If you still feel you would like not to come, please discuss directly with Dr. Cosgrove or the chief of staff." We didn't hear much after that.

We also wrote letters of appreciation to department administrators, department chairs, and institute chairs to thank them for their continued support of the effort and the facilitators. Here's an excerpt:

> John Smith is one of the 18 trained physician facilitators for this program.
>
> His role in this program has been invaluable, and the commitment that he has made to help our colleagues improve their skills is having an important impact on changing the culture of this organization.
>
> As of December, this group of 18 physicians has trained 509 staff members in this daylong, behavior-based communication training curriculum. This is an important achievement that we should all be proud of.
>
> Thank you for the contribution of your staff member to this very important program for our organization.

You barely get the words out about what you've accomplished before questions about sustainability creep in (Table 2.4). We've approached this from every angle.

Advanced communication courses provide additional training for more in-depth topics and are readily available and taught by our same core facilitator team. We also offer individual peer communication skills coaching. Often, physicians will complete the FHC course but then look for more feedback, which individual coaching can provide. We review doctor communication measures in our annual professional staff reviews with a Board of Governors member, as well as with local leadership. Every quarter the entire institute leadership appears before the executive team and reports on their scorecards, which are a blend of experience, quality, and safety metrics. This also includes doctor communication as a target, so communication skills efforts are woven into our organizational fabric. We believe effective communication skills training must start in person and are exploring supplementing that with online training.

TABLE 2.4 **Sustainable Communication Skills Training**

Curriculum Design	• Advanced communication courses • Exclusive inpatient application of R.E.D.E. • Online training • "Booster shot" updates • Peer coaching • Leadership, quality, safety, and professionalism collaborations • Integration into onboarding
Accountability	• Report quarterly unblinded communication scores by individual. • Show communication performance online. • Hold regularly scheduled scorecard reviews with executive leadership. • Make communication a factor in annual performance review.
Facilitator Engagement	• Hold quarterly faculty development sessions. • Promote opportunities to present outside the organization. • Open access to a formalized Research Council. • Start an e-mail newsletter with updates and training opportunities. • Share resources with medical school. • Promote Empathy + Innovation Summit track design and course offerings.
Expansion to Specific Groups	• Offer malpractice discounts as incentive for course completion. • Design a nursing curriculum. • Design specialty-specific programs.

We've also designed disease- and setting-specific training. Many of the communication models are geared for the outpatient setting, and not all providers naturally make the connection as to how these skills play out in the inpatient environment, so we built training specific to that space. In addition, there are nuances to conversations that are disease-specific. Discussing topics such as death by neurological criteria and end of life is done best when clinicians have a strong foundation of relationship-centered communication skills upon which additional skills can be layered.

Data

We thought about data a few different ways, and this was important to our success. If asked to build a communication skills training program, follow that invitation with a question about what you will be held accountable for. Spreading out the metrics helps capture the full impact of any training on a given clinician. We followed HCAHPS and CGCAHPS, but we knew that we also wanted to incorporate the clinicians' perspective on their own empathy, resilience, and confidence to perform the skills. We assessed empathy and burnout using the Jefferson Scale of Empathy (JSE) and the Maslach Burnout Inventory (MBI) respectively. We used the 12-month visit-specific CGCAHPS survey because it maps directly to a given provider. In an early analysis, we asked 897 attending physicians about their confidence in performing certain skills before and after the course. The results appear in Table 2.5.

As for the provider perceptions of the course itself:

- 88.2 percent were satisfied with R.E.D.E. duration
- 98 percent appreciated the teaching methods used
- 97.7 percent were satisfied/very satisfied with R.E.D.E. overall
- 94.7 percent would recommend R.E.D.E. to a friend or colleague

In the early analysis, empathy significantly increased according to the JSE from 116 to 124. Burnout significantly decreased as measured on the MBI from 65 to 62. And physician communication improved significantly in 6 out of 7 CGCAHPS questions.

A controlled study of the impact of the R.E.D.E. to Communicate: FHC course on burnout, empathy, confidence, and patient satisfaction has recently been published.[2] We also created an IRB-approved registry for all clinicians who completed our course and are working to link communication and these scales to disease-specific outcomes and correlate it to patient complaints and cost.

TABLE 2.5 **Physician Self-Efficacy Pre- and Post-FHC Training: "Extremely Confident" Responses**

FACTOR	PRE (N = 897)	POST (N = 897)	P-value
Phase 1	412 (50.2)	587 (75.1)	<0.001[a]
Respect with Welcome*	411 (46.0)	572 (70.1)	<0.001[a]
Set Agenda*	298 (33.6)	468 (57.4)	<0.001[a]
Introduce Computer*	175 (21.2)	386 (49.6)	<0.001[a]
Empathy*	418 (46.9)	535 (65.6)	<0.001[a]
Phase 2	407 (45.9)	587 (72.0)	<0.001[a]
Reflective Listening*	329 (36.8)	506 (62.0)	<0.001[a]
Eliciting Patient Narrative*	357 (40.1)	511 (62.7)	<0.001[a]
Explore Patient Perspective*	271 (30.5)	457 (55.9)	<0.001[a]
Phase 3	429 (49.2)	609 (75.4)	<0.001[a]
Sharing Diagnosis*	397 (44.6)	544 (67.7)	<0.001[a]
Develop Treatment Plan*	361 (41.1)	506 (62.4)	<0.001[a]
Provide Closure*	248 (28.1)	464 (57.1)	<0.001[a]
Dialogue vs. Monologue*	257 (28.9)	439 (53.9)	<0.001[a]

*Data not available for all subjects. Values presented as N (column %).
p-values: a = McNemar test

Getting Started

Here are a few things to consider when thinking about embarking on training:

Timing: If you train clinicians as facilitators and they don't use their skills, those skills will atrophy and die. A meaningful investment in communication skills training must occur at the same time your organization is actually ready to make it happen. If you are still having conversations about whether you should unblind your individual communication scores to the caregivers, then you may not be ready to launch a program. Behavior change and appetite for communication skills training will be driven by unblinded transparency of communication scores.

Cost: An eight-day TTT program—even one day of training—is a significant commitment of resources. People often ask about the cost. Our preferred response is, "What's the cost of not doing it? How do you capture that?" We looked at how patients perceived their providers' ability to communicate and mapped it to lawsuits and cost: physicians with the lowest communication scores have the highest number of lawsuits filed against them and cost our organization the most money. Multiple studies have confirmed the link of ineffective communication and malpractice risk.[3] In addition, continuing medical education (CME) accreditation is an attractive benefit to factor in when considering cost.

Consistency: Maintaining consistency in a program involves ongoing faculty development. We bring our facilitators together every quarter to discuss pertinent issues for our center and facilitation challenges and successes, as well as to expand their skill sets. We'll bring in outside speakers with communication skills expertise or share skills we've learned from across the globe. We also observe our facilitators regularly to give them feedback on their facilitation skills.

Program: We evolved external training in response to external demand. It wasn't our intention when we started. There are many groups that offer Train the Trainer programs, some effective and some probably less so. We've had some organizations say, "We started with X, and it didn't work. Can you come in and help us fix it?" This is tricky because if the audience is full of healthy skeptics and the program is not of high quality, then people develop "antibodies" and increased resistance to future training. Invest in getting it right the first time.

Data: Ask for data. What evidence do you have that a training program worked? Anecdotal quotes are great, but where is the meat? Saying this is the right thing to do may work for some, but it won't work for all. Meaningful impact must be demonstrated.

Culture: Is your organization ready for communication skills training? Do you have leadership support both verbally and financially? What efforts have you tried already, and do you have antibodies to work through? What is the motivation to get started, and how has this been messaged to date? Would interprofessional or peer-to-peer training work better at your institution?

Today

We started with six people and ultimately grew a Center for Excellence in Healthcare Communication (CEHC) (Figure 2.1), which is within our Office of Patient Experience and sponsored by the chief experience officer. The CEHC runs the R.E.D.E. to Communicate: FHC course, the advanced

FIGURE 2.1 **The Center for Excellence in Healthcare Communication**

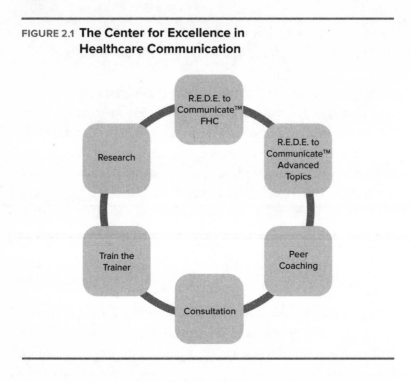

communication curriculum, a peer coaching program, a consulting arm, a comprehensive Train the Trainer (TTT) program for facilitators, and research. Several of these pieces will be discussed in subsequent chapters.

Key programmatic accomplishments:

1. Over four years, we trained 4,263 physicians and 840 advanced care providers in relationship-centered communication skills.
2. There are 56 clinician facilitators who lead the FHC program and advanced courses, of whom a third are surgeons, a third are medical staff, and a third are advanced care providers.
3. The R.E.D.E. model has been integrated into the medical school as a unifying curriculum across the professional continuum.

4. The R.E.D.E. to Communicate: FHC course is mandatory for onboarding of new physician staff.

When we first started to evaluate the course, we were not very sophisticated. We were most excited that it was rolling out the door. Perhaps the most powerful lesson we learned, which also transformed what we attempted to capture in the course, was that there can be two goals in teaching relationship-centered communication skills: (1) To deliver more or new content. Educators call this *informative*. A good analogy is adding water to a bucket. (2) To transform the bucket itself, perhaps into a boat. This is called *transformative*. We knew we were on to something when we started receiving feedback from participants:

> Really first rate and a game changer in terms of my practice.
>
> —NEUROSURGEON

> This course was a great tool for focusing on clarity and compassion in communication.
>
> —ANONYMOUS

> Just a big shout-out from me on your teaching at the course today. I have been so curious as to the content/delivery of the communications course, having discussed it from so many perspectives all year. FYI: it clearly exceeded my expectations.
>
> —RHEUMATOLOGIST

> This has been so far one of the best things in my career I've done.
>
> —CICU INTENSIVIST

Power Points

1. Complete an inventory of what already exists in your organization as a critical first step.

2. Identify relevant stakeholders who will impact your success or failure.

3. Unblinded and public transparency of patient satisfaction scores highlights opportunities for improvement, but be cautious about how you use them. Scores alone typically don't inspire people.

4. Choose facilitators who reflect the composition of your actual organization and who have a sphere of influence and are passionate about the initiative.

5. Changing the behavior, through your training, of even one person who has a large sphere of influence can have a powerful ripple effect throughout your organization.

Keys to Launching a Successful Communication Skills Training Program

wo of the underlying challenges facing anyone developing a healthcare communication skills training
program for clinicians are legitimacy and credibility.
A polarity exists in medicine between the positions that
quality medicine is about technique and biomedical understanding, on the one hand, and that quality medicine is a
humanistic endeavor in which emotional intelligence and
communication and relationship skills are important, on the
other. Although these two positions are not mutually exclu-
sive, they are often posed as if they were, as though we had to
choose between having an airline pilot who knew how to take
off or one who knew how to land. During training, physicians
primarily receive feedback on medical knowledge, decision
making, and procedural skills. Suddenly holding them

accountable for communication and interpersonal skills can feel like changing the rules halfway through the game.

A different version of these challenges comes from clinicians who believe that they are excellent communicators who do not need communication skills training. They may have strong interpersonal skills and great charisma and have warm relationships with their patients. They may have been practicing medicine for over a decade. Who are we to tell them how to do their jobs? How safe is it for them to consider that there is room for improvement in how they communicate with patients?

Resistance is to be expected. Be prepared for skepticism and pushback, and make a genuine effort to respond to resistance empathically from a perspective of curiosity and understanding. After all, skepticism is a prized quality in scientists, whom we expect to question and challenge ideas as a way of testing their validity. We show our colleagues respect by empathizing with the stress caused by both the changing measures of what represents high-quality healthcare and by the perception that their skills are being questioned. We show respect by welcoming their skepticism that communication skills can be taught effectively. A key to the success of our program was our expectation that very few clinicians would want to take our communication skills course and that many of those attending the course would reject what we were trying to teach. We will discuss later in this chapter why we made the choices we made and detail our various attempts to respond to this challenging environment.

How We Structured Our Course

Our basic framework for the course was to present a brief didactic on one of three phases of the medical interview followed by a brief demonstration of the skills for that phase and a longer period for skills practice. The didactic was given to provide a cognitive framework so that we could set up participants to succeed during the skills practice. For the first two phases, participants played both the patient and the clinician, whereas for the third phase, we originally employed standardized patients. At the end of the course, we spent 90 minutes practicing the skills on challenging cases that participants described from their own practices. The goal of this final component was to create an opportunity for participants to discover how the skills we had practiced could be applied in their specific practices and to highlight to participants that the model applied to challenging cases—new skills were not necessary to navigate most of these conversations. Because we could only practice a couple of cases in the time we had, we elicited a case from each participant and then had the group vote on which ones they wanted to recreate, with the person who supplied the case playing the role of the patient and a volunteer playing the clinician. This was important because the patient was played by someone who had spent time with him or her and because it encouraged the clinician to develop a more empathic understanding of the patient. We would later change this format to make the case more universal and enhance group buy-in.

Each session of the course, both in its initial Four Habits structure and subsequently using the R.E.D.E. model, had 8 to 12 participants and two facilitators. For the skills practice exercises for each phase, participants were divided into two groups of four to six, so that each participant would be able to practice at least two of the phases during the course. For the final session using cases supplied by and voted on by the group, we brought all the participants together again.

The participants in each course were drawn from a variety of specialties. We intentionally avoided having sessions that were dominated by a single department or subspecialty due to our concern that a tribal dynamic might develop that would strengthen resistance. We discovered that participants expressed great appreciation for the opportunity to meet colleagues whom they had not known previously, so we had little incentive to change this policy of diversity. In fact, we decided that no more than four physicians from the same specialty could attend at any one time. There was also diversity with regard to communication skills. Having some highly skilled communicators as participants helped us because they served as unofficial cofacilitators and modeled skills for others. In addition, we avoided creating the impression that the course was remedial.

What Works in Communication Skills Training?

Our initial question when we started to build our program was, what was known about the effectiveness of different approaches to teaching communication skills? Numerous studies had been published over the preceding decades that tested a variety of strategies, some of which focused on clinicians, while others focused on patients.[1] Most describe small numbers of physicians in general practice or oncology. Others focused on medical outcomes and demonstrated that communication skills training for either doctors or patients could improve measurable medical outcomes such as blood glucose levels and blood pressure.[2] Communication skills and communication skills training have both been associated with higher patient satisfaction.[3] Not surprisingly, some educational approaches have been shown to work better than others.[4] Also noteworthy is the relatively small number of studies employing rigorous study design.[5]

When we reviewed the published literature on communication skills training, several key themes emerged. The first was that experiential learning and skills practice were key.[6] Studies of didactic interventions that relied on cognitive learning showed no impact on future communication behavior. The implication of the data was that communicating well was more about skill than understanding. Like any skill, whether it's playing tennis or the violin or building a wooden cabinet, it was necessary to break down the larger process into key core elements and practice them with opportunities for skilled feedback. We learned the key distinction between understanding how to communicate and being able to communicate. Just as the test of violinists is how well they play rather than how much they know, so, too, the key communication skills question is how well someone communicates. In our early courses, we saw this in physicians who could define empathy and articulate its importance but struggled to make an empathic statement. In building our program, we therefore concentrated on providing the best opportunities for skill acquisition and practice and tried to minimize the time spent on cognitive learning. Our primary challenge was to change behaviors rather than to increase knowledge.

While this insight came initially from reviewing published studies, it also had face validity. Many of the communication errors that clinicians make can hardly be attributed to lack of understanding. Take, for example, studies that have documented an absence of empathy from clinicians. One finding is that, when faced with an upset patient, physicians often change the subject to something less emotionally charged, such as the medication list or past medical history, a phenomena known as blocking.[7] Is it really plausible that physicians have a thoughtfully constructed theory that what a crying patient needs is to be distracted by changing the subject? Or is it more likely that crying patients make physicians uncomfortable, we don't like to feel uncomfortable, and we lack a skilled empathic response, so we try to make the crying stop?

Is the problem that clinicians don't know what to do or that they don't know how to do it? The patient's distress provokes not an idea but a feeling in the clinician. Being and staying with a patient who is displaying strong emotion and learning to feel competent responding to that distress requires practice for most people. We expect a surgeon to use well-honed techniques to skillfully manage a bleeding artery, and address it directly. Yet the same event would cause panic in a medical student. Practice can help clinicians overcome their own internal distress in the presence of strong patient emotions and learn to respond in a calm and caring manner.

However, practice is not enough.

> *Without skilled feedback from people they trust, most clinicians have a hard time refining their skills.*

Clinicians are practicing communication skills every time they interact with a patient, but they are not receiving feedback in a way that can help them to improve. They may know that some patients are highly satisfied while others are not, but they have little if any data about which specific behaviors are resulting in which outcomes.

Adult Learning Theory and Small Group Facilitation Skills

While reviewing evidence-based components of a successful program, a second key influence on us was adult learning theory. We planned to educate attending physicians first before moving on to nurse practitioners, physician assistants, and physicians in residency and fellowship training programs.

We knew that we would be working with professionals who, in many instances, had been in practice for at least a decade and that there was a risk that they would perceive us as telling them how to do their jobs. For these and other reasons, we designed our program to respect Knowles's six principles of adult learning.[8] These principles are that adults:

1. Are internally motivated and self-directed
2. Bring life experiences and knowledge to learning experiences
3. Are goal-oriented
4. Are relevancy-oriented
5. Are practical
6. Like to be respected

We anticipated that we would increase resistance if we made participants feel that we were imposing ideas or techniques on them or defining for them the key challenges that they faced. This led to an emphasis on developing a learner-centered approach in which participants would help set the agenda, decide what cases would be practiced, and develop solutions to the problems that were presented or that emerged in the course of the class. By asking them to identify the sorts of patient scenarios that represented communication challenges for them, we allowed them to be self-directed, we respected their life experience, we tied the work to their goals, we made it relevant to their work, and we showed them respect. By emphasizing skills practice rather than didactics, we made the course practical. By facilitating a process by which the group of participants developed their own solutions to challenges, we showed respect for their intelligence and their experience. And because most clinicians dislike role-playing, we specifically referred to it as "skills practice" to emphasize the purpose rather than the activity.

Working in this way, however, required learning many skills related to small group facilitation. Historically, most medical education has been based on a model of the expert disseminating knowledge to the less expert. Lectures and highly hierarchical apprenticeship experiences predominated. The learners watched the expert and tried to model their own behavior on what they observed. In communication skills training of attending physicians, we did not think such a model was appropriate, nor was it likely to be accepted by participants. Our participants had extensive experience and their own wisdom. They had developed practical, if not optimal, approaches to the challenges that they faced. Providing a context in which they could reflect upon their challenges with a group of experienced colleagues and consider alternative approaches seemed more promising than telling them to do things differently: we aimed to facilitate learning rather than teach. In our judgment, our having expertise in how to communicate effectively was less important than having expertise in how to facilitate small groups so that an effective learning environment could be created. Our primary goal became fostering the formation of an effective group that could teach itself. In that way, we envisioned the communication skills course that we were developing not so much as a classroom but rather as a tumor board where different perspectives could be heard and a collective wisdom could emerge. One benefit of this approach was that it eliminated many sources of pushback: if we weren't setting the agenda and we weren't providing solutions, there was less to resist. By asking participants to come up with their own solutions, we were respecting them as professionals and encouraging them to take responsibility for their own learning and for the development of as high a level of competency as they were capable of achieving.

Keys to Small Group Communication Skills Training Facilitation

1. Express curiosity about and interest in participants.

2. Use facilitators who have credibility with participants.

3. Attend to group formation by making everyone feel welcome and using icebreakers and check-ins.

4. Use participants' past experience when building the agenda.

5. Establish ground rules (e.g., confidentiality, respect all opinions, silence, and put away all electronic devices).

6. Assess learners' goals.

7. Foster an appreciative environment focused on reinforcing feedback relevant to learners' goals.

8. Allow participants to make their own discoveries, draw their own conclusions, and come up with their own answers.

Creating an effective small group learning environment required several specific steps (see box). First, we didn't want to be told that we didn't understand the challenges that clinicians faced, so we only recruited facilitators who were busy clinicians themselves. Second, we were not focused on patient satisfaction scores in developing the course and were wary of being perceived as agents assigned to improve scores, so we emphasized the relevance of communication skills to quality medical care and to physician experience. We asked participants to reflect on their own positive experiences with the healthcare system when they were patients

Keys to Making Skills Practice Fun and Effective

1. Set clear ground rules:

   a. The person in the driver's seat can take a time-out to reflect or ask for help.

   b. The facilitator can take a time-out to make teaching points.

   c. Feedback, including self-assessment, starts with what was done effectively before addressing opportunities for improvement.

   d. Feedback starts with self-assessment by the person in the driver's seat before others provide feedback.

   e. Experimentation is encouraged and imperfection is expected.

   f. Skills practice has a time limit.

2. Bring an attitude of exploration, experimentation, and adventure.

3. Make it relevant to the learners' goals.

4. Do warm-up activities to help loosen up participants so that they can enter a more playful space and get into character.

or family members of patients. Third, we established ground rules that were reviewed at the beginning of each course that encouraged active participation, confidentiality, openness to different opinions, and silencing of electronic devices. The last item is important: having people on their smartphones during the course would have been distracting and prevented full engagement by the group as a whole, so participants were asked if they were expecting any urgent calls or e-mails that couldn't wait until the next break time. If they said no, then we established an expectation that phones and other devices would be put away. Fourth, we developed warm-ups and check-ins to facilitate the formation of relationships among the different participants. Warm-ups involve a series of crafted questions and exercises to gradually move people to a more creative and playful space, from left brain to right brain, which is essential to immersion in this training experience. Rest assured, they can go back across the corpus callosum in a little while.

At a broader level, we worked to foster an effective learning environment by creating a strongly positive and appreciative climate within the course. Much of the medical world is defined by deficit-based thinking. When a medical imaging study shows nothing bad, we say that the study is negative. When it shows a cancer, we say the test is positive. When no disease or abnormalities are found on a history or examination, we call it "unremarkable." We often only start filling in details when we find markers that herald disease. In some senses we stay quiet when all is healthy and only speak up when we find pathology. This culture carries over into the educational and interprofessional environments. People associate feedback with criticism, which isn't what effective feedback really is. When everyone is doing his or her job well, we are quiet. When people know what they are supposed to know, we take it for granted. We speak up when there is a mistake, a complication, or when someone answers a question incorrectly. This creates an environment where the priority becomes avoiding looking ignorant or foolish, and this can stifle creativity and experiential learning.

Our prioritization of overcoming the hypercritical environment of the hospital led to specific feedback strategies.

1. Structure feedback to be primarily supportive and reinforcing, aiming to give four times as much reinforcing feedback as corrective feedback.
2. Ask for learners' goals and focus feedback on areas they have identified as being of interest to them.
3. Have the participants reflect on their own performance, starting with what has been done effectively, followed by reinforcing feedback from others, before moving to self-reflection on what could have been done more effectively and modifying feedback from others.
4. Be careful not to overload participants with excessive feedback by asking them "How is this landing on you?" or "How are you feeling about the amount of feedback at this point?"

In this manner, we aimed to create an environment in which learners felt supported and felt that the group was looking for the best in them. Additional steps designed to create an appreciative environment included warmly welcoming participants at the beginning of the day and getting to know them over breakfast prior to the start of the class; warm-up exercises at the beginning of the class so that the participants could learn about each other; ample food and beverages so that participants felt cared for; and an eagerness to hear their opinions and solutions before or instead of offering our own.

Organizational Strategies for Success

Many of the steps described above seemed critically important to enhancing buy-in through effective facilitation: working in a learner-centered way on challenges that they identified, attention to group formation, creating a safe learning environment, respecting their experience as clinicians, and fostering an appreciative climate. However, there were other key elements more related to organizational strategy, which was more about leveraging communication skills training as a means to engage physicians. In many ways, Cleveland Clinic's history and Patients First laid the groundwork for us.

One was maintaining sensitivity to local culture and expectations. Cleveland Clinic grew out of a multispecialty group practice and is still in many ways a physician-run healthcare organization. Unlike some academic medical centers, high-quality clinical care is the highest priority of the institution, and busy clinicians with expertise are highly respected regardless of whether they publish a lot of papers or bring in external grant money. Our decision to recruit only busy clinicians as communication skills training facilitators was partly a reflection of our culture in which clinicians are highly esteemed. We believed that participants would be most open to reflecting on communication challenges with colleagues who also spent a significant amount of time seeing patients and confronting the hassles, annoyances, and inefficiencies that often exist in patient care settings. In a different hospital, it's entirely possible that clinicians would be more interested in working with people with a doctoral degree in education or psychology who brought specific academic credentials certifying them as qualified to teach communication skills. Sensitivity and responsiveness to local culture increases the likelihood of buy-in.

Second, we sought as much voluntary participation in the course as possible and knew that busy clinicians were unlikely to decide spontaneously that they wanted to spend a day in a communication skills training course. We knew that when we first started teaching the course, our skill level as facilitators would not yet be well developed. Yet when a new program is rolled out, it typically gets the most attention in the early days, when kinks are being worked out and new faculty are getting up to speed and developing their expertise. The first sessions will not go as smoothly as desired. Unexpected challenges arise, and facilitators learn to adjust to the variations that occur from group to group. If the first few sessions go badly and word gets out that the course is not a good product, support and participation can evaporate quickly. Just as theatrical productions on Broadway often start with runs in smaller cities where the kinks can be ironed out away from the limelight, so too did we think it important to start our work in an environment in which it was safe to have a few failures while we figured out what we were doing. We addressed these challenges by asking friends and colleagues whom we knew to be effective communicators and to have a strong interest in communication skills to participate in the early sessions of the course. We asked them to give us feedback so that we could improve. By doing so, we earned constructive criticism and support rather than word-of-mouth sabotage. The result was a kind of stealth marketing campaign whereby the friendly early participants went back to their various departments and divisions and told their colleagues what a wonderful course it was. This led to rapid escalation of participation in the course, and by the time that happened, we had had substantial practice and had developed confidence and poise as facilitators. When the course was made mandatory for all physicians, it had a strong reputation as being a high-quality and relevant experience.

A third critical element enhancing buy-in was strong commitment from the highest levels of leadership at Cleveland Clinic. There were strong endorsements of the course at staff meetings, and generous resources (i.e., time) were provided to support the work. The leadership support occurred in the context of a broader and more comprehensive effort to improve patient experience and to make all hospital employees see patient experience as a priority. This made the emphasis on communication skills training more credible and positioned it as a key element of the larger institutional mission. Hospital leaders further signaled their belief in the importance of communication skills training by having the entire executive leadership team take the course, including colleagues in financial, human relations, and operational leadership roles.

A fourth organizational strategy was investing in our facilitators to make them effective, as well as to build a strong cadre, which we believed would reward us in the long term. Preparing trainers to work in this manner where they are facilitating learning rather than teaching, reflecting questions and resistance back to the group, and creating an appreciative and safe environment requires substantial time and training. Facilitators need practice to achieve competency. There is a steep learning curve, and we invested time and effort in observing our facilitators in action and holding regular faculty development sessions.

Finally, time is precious in the healthcare environment and must be addressed by the organization. Hospitals and practices are running on ever-tighter budgets, and clinicians and administrators face increasing pressure to maximize revenue by seeing as many patients as possible. Pulling clinicians out of clinical work for communication skills training means lost revenue in the short run with no guarantee that it will be made up in the long run. A frequent response to this problem is to propose that clinicians have an early morning or lunchtime lecture on how to communicate effectively, an approach that has been shown not to work. Just as people cannot learn to ski or play tennis by attending a one-hour lecture or a long series of lectures, nor can people learn to communicate more effectively with such an approach.[9] Learning new skills requires opportunities to practice. We designed our course to last a full day because we discovered that we needed at least that much time to include meaningful skills practice and because we could not realistically ask for more. It also took time for the small groups to coalesce into a coherent and trusting team in which participants felt safe enough to participate effectively in role-plays. It's hard for that to happen in an hour. Anyone preparing a communication skills course needs to be prepared to ask for sufficient course time to accomplish meaningful work. Changing human behavior is difficult and cannot be done quickly and cheaply. Outcomes studies of communication skills training initiatives report that in order to be effective, programs should last at least one day.[10]

Overcoming Resistance to Skills Practice

If you walk into a room of physicians and ask them for volunteers to participate in a communication skills training course, you will find few raised hands. If you mention that the course will include role-playing, most people will leave the room as quickly as possible. And yet our experience has been that many of our participants have requested additional opportunities to continue practicing their skills using role-play exercises. Why do role-play exercises have such a bad reputation? How does one make them fun and productive?

When role-plays go wrong, the etiology can usually be tracked to a facilitator who is not prepared, skilled, and fully comfortable working with physicians. We are not saying that people don't have the best of intentions; we are saying that teaching communication skills is complex, high-risk work, and it should be thoughtfully planned and meticulously executed. Role-playing is a vulnerable place for most people to be; participants should be handled with appropriate care.

For example, leaders of one major hospital system that invited us to work with them reported that when they sent a faculty member to their simulation center for remedial training in communication skills, she walked out of the session in tears because she felt so humiliated. Trainees who participated in communication skills training role-plays at the same center rebelled and refused to continue their participation. And yet when we ran sessions for them, we found that, by the end, the trainees were volunteering to participate in our "skills practice." Similarly, attending national conferences throughout our careers, we have seen that the typical role-play scenario involves pairing up with someone who happens to be sitting next to you and practicing specific scenarios with no skilled observer present to provide feedback. No structure is provided to help people identify what they are doing effectively and what they should consider doing differently. It's like playing the piano without being able to hear anything.

Other scenarios involve bringing people up in front of a group to play a role without preparing participants to succeed in their assigned roles. Sometimes it's not clear which skills they are supposed to practice or demonstrate. Sometimes they've been given inadequate preparation to assume the assigned role. Often the agenda is set entirely by the teacher with no input from the learner about what he wants to work on. Feedback often is provided in the typical deficit-based manner where shortcomings are highlighted and less attention is given to what was done effectively. The experience of participants is that they are placed in an exposed position, asked to perform a task not of their choosing and for which they feel inadequately prepared, and then criticized for anything that they do ineffectively in front of an audience. Who would volunteer for such an experience? We wouldn't, and we're pretty sure you wouldn't either.

What we realized was that we could only succeed with skills practice if we were highly conscientious about establishing a process that was safe, constructive, and relevant to the participants' goals and work. And we wanted to make it fun. A key element here is working hard to prepare participants to succeed so that feedback can focus on reinforcing their success. Setting people up to fail and then giving them feedback on their failure is mean and counterproductive, not to mention the kiss of death for your program.

Making skills practice safe requires very specific steps. First, there need to be ground rules so that participants know what to expect. We allow the participant practicing a skill to pause at any time if he or she feels stuck or wants to talk through what is happening or what to do next. We ask the participant to tell us what he or she wants to work on and get feedback about and then focus on those issues. We clearly define the skill that we want participants to practice and make sure that they have a plan for what to do before they begin. We take careful notes so that we can give feedback on specific behaviors and word choices, and we avoid evaluative language. Telling a participant, "The patient seemed to start to calm down when you said, 'I know your time is valuable, and I can understand why you would be angry about having to wait so long,'" is more helpful than "You did a great job calming the patient down." We work hard to eliminate language such as "good/bad," "liked/didn't like," and "great" and replace it with "effective/less effective"—the former has a value judgment, while the latter does not. In addition, we always start feedback by having the participants in the role-play reflect on their own performance, beginning with what they did effectively. When observers give feedback, they also must start with what was done effectively. This creates, as noted previously, a culture in which people feel confident that others are looking for the best in them and giving them credit for their successes. Ninety-eight percent of physicians are challenged by this and usually start phrases with "I did well at ____, but I didn't do ____ and ____ and ____." This pervasive tendency requires active facilitation. In such a supportive environment, people become more willing to take risks, try new things, and be open about where they think they can improve.

A related issue is the defensiveness that arises when clinicians perceive criticism that they are poor or unskilled communicators. This is not to be taken lightly or underestimated. Because all caregivers are deeply invested in the care they provide, phrases such as "your scores are low" or "I wouldn't have said . . ." can be interpreted as a criticism of them as a person and caregiver, which puts them at high risk for being emotionally hijacked. They then worry more about protecting themselves than about learning.

One agenda that participants often suspect is that communication skills training is designed to improve patient satisfaction scores and that participants are selected if they are considered poor communicators. The implied agenda is that we are there to fix them. The key problem here is that it is very hard for people to learn when they feel defensive. If they feel criticized and overly stressed, they are more inclined to show you how much they already know rather than to learn new things. Defensive participants also tend to focus on all the shortcomings of any alternative way of communicating because they are invested in justifying their current practices. Actively displaying abundant respect for and appreciation of the skills and experience of participants was essential in our work. When the participants perceived that we admired them and were not there to remediate, their need to defend themselves diminished and they became more open to experimenting and learning.

Some communication skills programs focus exclusively on reinforcing feedback. We chose to give both reinforcing and modifying feedback to enhance credibility and authenticity with physicians. No one is perfect; there is always something that could be more effective. Our goal is not to hide from this reality but rather to create an environment in which carefully chosen opportunities for improvement can be explored safely. By the same token, we reject the feedback sandwich in which criticism is surrounded before and after with praise; everyone knows that a sandwich is primarily defined by what's in the middle, and the praise can come across as perfunctory. This raises a key point: reinforcing feedback must be sincere and specific, and facilitators must therefore develop finely tuned observational skills so that they notice and can identify effective behaviors upon which they can comment. Many of us have tuned our eyes and ears to focus on mistakes and imperfections, and this bias must be conscientiously unlearned.

The notion that role-plays can be fun may sound naive, but our experience indicates otherwise. The word "play" in role-play is often overlooked, yet making role-plays playful is key to their success. An important issue here that extends well beyond the issue of role-plays is agenda setting. One of the reasons we think that communication skills training in general and role-play exercises in particular generate so much resistance is that the participants experience someone else's agenda being imposed upon them. The teacher has drawn a path and now expects the students to walk it. Adult learners resist being controlled in this manner. We did not want to be salespeople pushing a product. We wanted to invite people into a fun and productive environment where they could try some new things to help them with challenges in their work lives.

One alternative to walking a predefined path is going on an adventure. If a communication skills course can be viewed as a learning laboratory, then the task is to experiment with new things and discover what happens. As with a scientific laboratory, the key question isn't so much who's right and who's wrong but what did we learn from the last experiment and what would be a logical next step. Approaching such work with a sense of curiosity and wonder, an openness to the many different approaches that can be applied to any given communication challenge, feels very different from arriving with a set of hoops through which participants are expected to jump.

Similarly, although we had defined what we viewed to be a key set of core communication skills, we strove to present these skills as options to be tried and tested so that participants could decide for themselves what worked for them. And if they wanted to experiment with their own alternative approaches, we encouraged them to do so. We believe that their own experience and feedback from other participants would be far more persuasive than anything we could say. This turned out to be quite true. Physicians most valued the feedback from the patient, followed by their peers and then the facilitator.

Power Points

1. Credibility and validity will be issues when creating communication skills programs. Anticipate skepticism and resistance and be prepared to meet them with empathic curiosity.

2. Communication skills programs must include experiential learning (as opposed to passive didactics), be rooted in adult learning theory, and last one day or more.

3. Do facilitate; don't lecture. Create opportunities for participants to make their own discoveries rather than spoon-feeding them yours. Leverage the expertise of your group for maximal engagement.

4. Invest in faculty development for facilitators. Feedback skills are critical.

5. Be on the lookout for emotionally hijacked learners. Show participants the same empathy you hope they will show patients.

6. Start by knowing your culture, securing leadership endorsement and resources for facilitator training, and clarifying time coverage.

7. Begin small, and do not try to grow the program until it is working effectively. Test and develop the initial offering with friendly, known participants before opening it to others.

8. Appreciation, safety, fun, and setting participants up for success are critical to optimal learning in skills practice.

Birth of the
R.E.D.E.™ Model

Whatever the nature of our wounds,
we heal to be healed.

—ANTHONY SUCHMAN AND
DALE MATTHEWS[1]

ealthcare providers go into medicine to help alleviate
human suffering. Though medical training quickly
zeroes in on building biomedical knowledge and
expertise, relationships are essential to our health and well-
being as well as to our basic survival. Cozolino asserts that we
are all social beings, developing relationships on multiple levels "from neurons to neighborhoods."[2] We are shaped from
birth by our dependency on others to meet our basic physical
and psychological needs. We quickly adapt—learning how
to interact with our environment and develop meaningful
relationships that activate development of brain structure and
biochemistry.[3] Should it be surprising then that these personal

connections play a vital role in our physical and emotional development and well-being? Meaningful relationships have been shown to be therapeutic, in and of themselves, resulting in improved health outcomes such as lower blood pressure, better pain management, and weight loss.[4] Mindful awareness and intentional practice of empirically validated and efficacious communication skills have the power to deepen our connections with others.

Healthcare providers feel deep responsibility in caring for people. Reversing a diagnosis that someone has had for years is delicate work. Getting patients to take medication when they don't believe it will be helpful is challenging. Rather than explore the patients' goals and motivations through meaningful dialogue, clinicians often try to convince patients to do what they want them to do. Perhaps as biomedical advances led providers to become increasingly specialized, the focus of the individual also narrowed. The inability to view the patient in his or her entirety has led many to feel disenfranchised and disengaged from their own care.[5]

At the same time, with increasing consumerism in healthcare, patient-centered care is commonly championed in today's healthcare environment. It has permeated the atmosphere of medicine. Patient-centered care and the inclusion of psychosocial elements in the biomedical framework have been valued increasingly as research unfolds to support a more holistic and humanistic view of disease, illness, and patient care.[6] One of our challenges in teaching communication skills is to address the disconnect between the doctor-centered, pathophysiology-based perspective and the more holistic, patient-centered perspective. As part of the R.E.D.E. to Communicate: FHC course, we ask providers to recall a positive healthcare interaction they've had *as a patient*. We then ask them to identify what it was that made the encounter powerful and memorable. Commonly, the stories speak of feeling cared for and valued. They express gratitude that the clinician took the time to get to know them as a person and to listen to and understand their concerns. When they find themselves in the role of patient, physicians value the experience of being seen as a human being. This should not be surprising. As healthcare providers, we have the power to connect and be present with patients in that dark, lonely space so often filled with fear, pain, and loss. Our willingness to meet patients in this space and walk alongside them can be therapeutic for all concerned.

Unfortunately, in the current climate of economic uncertainty, tightening budgets, and demands for increased productivity, the focus on patient-centered care has resulted in many clinicians themselves feeling disengaged. Pressure to make up for deficiencies in the current healthcare system, to improve access, efficiency, safety, and quality while completing extensive documentation that often seems irrelevant to improving their patients' outcomes or experience, with less time and fewer resources for the things they believe to be important, all contribute to dissatisfaction among providers. Providers also suffer from information overload with requests arriving via mail, e-mail, pager, smartphone, fax, and electronic medical record. The number of medical journals has exploded such that a new medical article is now published every 26 seconds; keeping up with a specialty requires increasing time and effort.[7] Consequently, we have learned to juggle many balls and to filter much of what comes at us. Unfortunately, this multitasking and selective attention clouds awareness and prevents us from being fully present in any moment, much less in one with a patient. A certain degree of stress can be healthy to motivate and achieve peak performance.[8] Too much stress, however, can lead to distress and burnout, and can render clinicians incapable of being mindfully present with patients, much less communicating effectively. When overburdened clinicians are asked to be more patient-centered and to attend more to patient experience, they may say, "Well, what about my experience?"

A Solution That Resonates with Clinicians and Patients

Relationship-centered care, and relationship-centered communication as the primary vehicle, bridges this dichotomy by shifting the focus and power to the relationship or personal connection between provider and patient.[9]

Relationships in healthcare extend far beyond that of patient-provider. Today, healthcare occurs among interdisciplinary teams and within the community at large. The Pew-Fetzer Task Force on Advancing Psychosocial Health Education established relationship-centered care to better recognize the value of these multilevel relationships and the unique perspective of each participant in caring for individual patients.[10] Building upon this formulation, Beach, Inui, and the Relationship-Centered Care Research Network outlined four major principles of relationship-centered care (RCC).[11]

The first principle is mutual respect. Both provider and patient are recognized and appreciated for their unique perspectives, experiences, and expertise.[12] As a provider, this is a blend of personal and professional culture, socialization, education, and practice. Patients present with personal expertise characterized by their experience of their illness, preexisting knowledge, life experience, and sociocultural upbringing. Tempering the historical power differential through mutual respect improves a patient's sense of efficacy.[13] Self-efficacy is a key component in one's readiness to change behavior whether it be taking insulin for diabetic management or acting on a referral for additional testing to rule out a malignancy.[14] A second characteristic of RCC is eliciting and understanding the psychosocial context in which the patient is experiencing a particular biomedical issue.[15] We must possess and convey genuine interest in the patient as a human being with individual thoughts, behaviors, and emotions. Without intentionality, such sentiments can easily go unvoiced due to time and task demands. Through exploration of the patient's perspective and psychosocial context, we can be more mindful of and attentive to the patient's needs and thus evolve our healthcare relationship. A third characteristic of RCC is acknowledgement of reciprocal influence. Though patients are the focus of healthcare relationships, both parties influence one another. Thus, as providers, we, too, can and often do derive benefit from relationships with our patients. Acknowledging how patients inspire, teach, and even care for us through respect and relationship can go a long way in a proactive and collaborative partnership to manage a patient's health. A fourth characteristic of RCC is the affirmation of genuine relationships as inherently valuable. The more care and connection providers feel toward patients, the more invested we are in their health and well-being. Similarly, patients who partner with a provider are more likely to feel efficacious in caring for themselves and yield greater levels of self-management and treatment adherence.[16]

Using relationship-centered care to improve patient *and* provider experience, we strove to offer opportunities in the course that might build resilience and offer respite for providers. We weren't just providing knowledge and skill building. We were providing an experience to our deserving, highly respected colleagues. Of primary significance, we related to providers in the same way we were asking them to connect with patients, conveying empathy, listening attentively, eliciting their perspectives, and valuing their contributions in an authentic and genuine manner.

We rolled out our initial pilot to 1,000 fairly skeptical yet just as friendly clinicians and were grateful for responses such as "a valuable use of time," "refreshing," "not what I expected," "helpful to know others experience similar challenges," and "I can actually use this." Still, we observed that when providers were practicing communication skills in our pilot course, many did not intuitively view "forming relationships" with patients as part of their role. Even those who wanted to connect with patients were often distracted by multitasking, information overload, and other challenges. This was concerning because we believed that providers and patients alike would not reap the full benefits of relationship-centered communication if they only applied the skills prescriptively or in a less than mindful way.[17]

Relationship as a Vital Change Agent

Several models have been developed to facilitate teaching and evaluation of healthcare communication.[18] The skills themselves are well known, and people have been studying relationship-centered care for a long time. Some wondered why another model was needed. What we wanted to do, however, was explicitly and concretely align our relationship-centered values and mission with the communication skills themselves, and to nudge providers to think differently about their roles in medicine. We also wanted a model that would transcend the outpatient setting and apply to any environment. This led us to develop a conceptual framework for teaching relationship-centered communication that we labeled the R.E.D.E. (pronounced "ready") model, which stands for Relationship Establishment, Development, and Engagement.

Based on the premise that a genuine relationship is a vital therapeutic agent, the R.E.D.E. model aims to improve the

TABLE 4.1 **R.E.D.E. to Communicate Model**

RELATIONSHIP:		
Establishment *Phase I*	**Development** *Phase II*	**Engagement** *Phase III*
• Convey value and respect with the welcome • Collaboratively set the agenda • Introduce the computer, if applicable • Demonstrate empathy using **S.A.V.E.** (**S**upport, **A**cknowledge, **V**alidate, **E**motion naming)	• Engage in reflective listening • Elicit the patient narrative • Explore the patient's perspective using **V.I.E.W.** (**V**ital activities, **I**deas, **E**xpectations, **W**orries)	• Share diagnosis and information • Collaboratively develop the plan • Provide closure • Dialogue throughout using **A.R.I.A.** (**A**ssess, **R**eflect, **I**nform, **A**ssess)

experience of both patient and provider. R.E.D.E. creates an intentional and reflective focus on the preeminence of relationship. As such, the R.E.D.E. model applies effective communication skills to optimize personal connections in three primary phases of Relationship: Establishment, Development, and Engagement (Table 4.1). R.E.D.E. harnesses the power of a relationship by using effective communication skills to focus on the essential features of each individual relationship.

One significant barrier had to be surmounted in developing and integrating R.E.D.E. into a new course called R.E.D.E. to Communicate: FHC. It pertained to the use of the word *relationship*, as it led to fears of being too touchy-feely for some or too presumptuous for others. Before clinicians were able to align with the principles of R.E.D.E., it was vital to define what a healthcare relationship was,[19] as well as what it wasn't (Table 4.2).

TABLE 4.2 **The Healthcare Relationship**

REQUIRED	NOT REQUIRED
• Emotional connection • Mutual respect • Genuine interest • Patient perspective and psychosocial context • Shared commitment to positive outcome	• Friendship • Agreement on everything • Unlimited time • Tolerance of boundary violations • Practice outside your usual scope

For instance, a healthcare relationship requires an emotional connection with patients, but it does not require friendship.[20] Whereas friends might spend a few hours conversing over a cup of coffee, providers don't have and are not expected to spend endless time developing healthcare relationships. We do not expect clinicians to always agree with patients nor to give them everything they want. Last, healthcare relationships don't require clinicians to compromise personal or professional boundaries. Boundaries are an important element in all relationships, and there are very clear and important boundaries in the patient-clinician relationship. If someone is being contemptuous or verbally assaulting, he or she is violating boundaries and the provider does not have to stand there and take it.

We wanted to create an environment wherein we were not simply teaching people skills, we were also challenging the way they thought. We were driving for cultural evolution. Our perspective on how healthcare relationships are defined within R.E.D.E. challenges users of the model to explore their own assumptions and beliefs about patients, their role as clinicians, and the ways in which they interact with other human beings. In this way, R.E.D.E. has the transformative power to stimulate and inform a provider's personal development and awareness. In addition, the model can be integrated with the traditional medical interview seamlessly (Table 4.3).

TABLE 4.3 **R.E.D.E. Model and the Traditional Medical Interview**

RELATIONSHIP:		
Establishment *Phase I*	**Development** *Phase II*	**Engagement** *Phase III*
• Identify chief complaint	• History of present illness • Past medical/social history • Meds and allergies • Family/social history, review of systems • Physical exam	• Diagnosis • Education • Shared decision making • Close
EMPATHY		

Our teaching of R.E.D.E. acknowledges and engages a clinician's expertise and encourages reflective competence, the notion that we are thinking about the words we speak and why we chose them, getting feedback on them, and revising our strategies accordingly.

The R.E.D.E. Model of Healthcare Communication

Phase I: Establish the relationship

Creating a safe and supportive atmosphere is essential for developing the trust necessary to establish a personal connection. The previous chapter details a significant amount of effort that went into making physicians feel safe; the same effort is required for patients.

The emotion bank account is a concept originally proposed by psychologist and author John Gottman, PhD. It refers to a mental system for tracking the frequency with which we emotionally connect with other people.[21] Each time an emotional connection is made, it is equivalent to making a deposit in the emotion account with that person. Building up the emotion account is important to sustain a personal connection. This way, when a withdrawal inevitably occurs, such as when a patient is forced to wait to see a provider, the emotion account does not automatically go into the red.

Convey value and respect with the welcome. In doing so, we are essentially building the emotion bank account with our patients and families. Given that people form first impressions quickly and patients are discussing emotional and value-laden topics, how we set the stage for conversation matters, even if it feels irrelevant to the clinical problems at hand.[22] The skills outlined in Phase I are intended to create a climate conducive to the development of trust by demonstrating that the provider is receptive and interested in the person first, patient second. For instance, while taking the time to review a patient's chart before meeting him or her increases clinical efficiency, intentionally sharing that we took this time provides additional value by conveying to the patient that we value his or her time and experiences. And if we don't tell patients we did it, then they don't know. "Thank you for choosing me" or "I'm glad you came into the ER" can go a very long way in a very short period of time. Knocking on the examination room door and confirming the correct patient and his or her readiness before entering the room further demonstrates a respect for patients' privacy and grants patients a small degree of control over their environment. Research has shown that a firm handshake and genuine smile help form a good first impression when culturally appropriate.[23] Another step in valuing the patient, and any companions present, is to exchange introductions, clarify roles, and attend to the patient's privacy. Positioning oneself at the patient's eye level and maintaining comfortable direct eye contact can reduce the power differential between provider and patient.

Arriving for a medical visit is not an isolated event but rather the culmination of a number of events that started with recognition that a problem is occurring, searching out the right provider, and scheduling and ended with getting to the actual appointment. Thus, it is essential to recognize and respond to any immediate signs of physical or emotional distress upon greeting the patient. In the absence of signs of distress, making a brief social comment related to the patient can help put him or her at ease and further build rapport. Giving patients an opportunity to talk about themselves apart from their illness can also convey respect for the patient as a person. Platt et al. assert that initiating nonemergent visits with new patients with, "Tell me about yourself . . ." is an effective strategy for conveying value and respect and building rapport.[24] Alternatively, we encourage messaging of what you value as a physician: "It's really important to me to learn more about you before we get started."

Collaboratively set the agenda. Many clinicians fear this practice will sacrifice time necessary for assessing or treating the primary concern. However, research has shown that sharing in agenda setting not only facilitates partnership but also improves visit efficiency, diagnostic accuracy, and patient satisfaction.[25] Shared agenda setting helps minimize our tendency to presume what a patient's concerns are and in what order of priority.

Since patients are generally not accustomed to this level of participation, it is important first to orient them to the goal of obtaining a complete list of presenting concerns in order to prioritize his or her needs. For example, "I'd like to get a list of all the things you'd like to address today so we can manage our time effectively" or "I know you came into the

ER with leg pain. What other concerns do you have?" Open-ended questions, such as, "What can I do for you?" followed by, "What else?" or "Is there something else?" are often necessary to elicit an exhaustive list.[26] Eliciting all of a patient's concerns early in the visit can be unsettling—more like terrifying—for clinicians who feel pressured for time. Despite the fears it often conjures, collaborative agenda setting has been shown to save time in the office visit.[27] Since a patient's outline of individual concerns might actually represent symptoms of an overarching diagnosis, having the list up front can increase efficiency and diagnostic accuracy. Last, although most physicians find mentioning time distasteful, it doesn't go away because we don't mention it. Time framing—"We have twenty minutes today . . ."—is a useful approach.

> *Collaborative agenda setting has been shown to save time in the office visit.*

In addition, patients do not always share the most important concern first, especially if it is very sensitive to the person.[28] Eliciting the full range of a patient's concerns early in the visit can reduce the potential for "doorknob questions,"[29] which adds time. Answering such questions can make the clinician late for subsequent patients, whereas failing to address them can result in patient harm or dissatisfaction; preventing them by eliciting all concerns early is a more effective strategy. Finally, if a patient raises an issue that is outside one's scope of practice, we are not, of course, expected to treat it. However, it is important to address the concern by referring the person to someone who can help and to message a willingness to hear it. The final skill is in adding your own agenda items, asking *patients* to prioritize their concerns, and then agreeing on what will be covered. For example, "So you came into the emergency department with chest pain. You said that the chest pain is your biggest concern, and you're also worried about your back pain. We can discuss both. I'd like to go over your test results, too. How does that sound?" If a patient identifies too many concerns to address in the time allotted, an example of an alternative is, "You have a number of concerns you'd like to address in our time together: chest pain, arthritis, and asthma. I agree that we should start with the chest pain. I want to do a thorough assessment, so if we don't cover everything we may need to find some more time in the near future. How does that sound?"

Introduce the computer. The electronic health record is a reality for most clinicians, and forming a relationship with a person who is staring at a screen, be it a computer, television, or smartphone, is challenging. To the extent possible, we should introduce and utilize the computer in a manner that enhances patient care rather than detracting from it.[30] Involving the patient in reviewing lab results or scans in his or her record, angling the screen to maximize direct eye contact, and a willingness to stop typing as soon as any hint of distress arises are important in minimizing the potential of the computer to cause disruption and alienation in the patient-clinician relationship.[31]

> *Empathy is the ability to imagine oneself in another's place and to express that imagining to the other person through communication.*

Demonstrate empathy. Academic definitions of empathy emphasize cognitive (detached concern), affective (emotional), moral (impulse to try to understand), and behavioral underpinnings (response through communication), which differentiate it from sympathy or compassion.[32]

Most clinicians care about their patients, but not all recognize emotional cues or respond to them.[33] Research shows that physicians respond to only one in 10 opportunities to express empathy.[34] Yet, verbal statements of empathy reduce the length of both an outpatient surgery and a primary care visit.[35] This makes sense. When someone is upset and receives an empathic response, he or she feels acknowledged and valued as a person. Empathy has also been shown to result in improved health outcomes such as improved control of low-density lipoprotein cholesterol and hemoglobin A1c in diabetic patients, shorter and less severe symptoms of the common cold, better pain management, and weight loss.[36] In R.E.D.E., every opportunity to convey empathy is encouraged, and the mnemonic S.A.V.E. (for Support, Acknowledge, Validate, and Emotion naming) is introduced for outlining different types of empathic statements a provider can use. Oftentimes clinicians have one or two ways of expressing empathy, and their arsenal can be expanded with S.A.V.E. Nonverbal behavior—such as a softer, lower tone of voice, a tilt of the head, or a hand over one's heart—are also powerful in communicating empathy. Having more options for conveying empathy verbally and nonverbally can allow us to tailor our response to the individual in an authentic and meaningful way.

Phase II: Develop the relationship

Once a safe and supportive environment has been created, the relationship needs to evolve and grow. Getting to know who the patient is as a person and understanding her or his symptoms in a biopsychosocial context is the next step.

Listen reflectively. Reflective listening is vital for developing the relationship and has been shown to enhance the therapeutic nature of a relationship, increase openness and the disclosure of feelings, and improve information recall.[37] Yet listening in such a way as to understand and acknowledge what is being said without interrupting or derailing the patient's train of thought can be challenging. Research has shown that physicians interrupt patients within 18 to 23 seconds of asking a question.[38] Attention and awareness are necessary to restrain the interruption reflex to redirect the conversation to where we would like to see it go. By attending to the facts, feelings, and intentions conveyed by the patient, we can respond reflectively and empathically without disrupting the patient's narrative.[39] This enables the patient to provide the details necessary for us to hear all of their concerns and thoughts as well as to better differentiate diagnoses.[40] Use of verbal continuers, such as "Mm-hmm" or "I see," and nonverbal continuers such as head nodding convey interest and attention without interrupting the patient. Being able to reflect back the underlying meaning or emotion being conveyed without judgment or distraction is especially valuable in deepening a shared understanding of the patient's perspective.

Elicit the patient narrative. Obtaining the history of present illness (HPI) can quickly become a series of closed-ended questions that are of most interest to the provider.[41] However, the goal of this skill is to use open-ended questions to better understand patients' perspectives on their condition. This has been proven more efficient and effective than a provider-centered data-gathering approach.[42] Examples include, "Now

I'd like to get a bird's-eye view of what has been going on with you" or "I'd like to learn as much as I can about your problem, from when it first began until now." Open-ended questions and verbal and nonverbal continuers are effective in maintaining the patient's narrative.

Elicit the patient's perspective. In healthcare, we tell patients things they don't want to hear. We give them news that will alter the course of their lives and those of their loved ones. How they react to and absorb these pieces of information is not just about the news itself but about all of their prior experiences, beliefs, and values. This unique perspective or "explanatory model" is one that we frequently don't know anything about.[43] Being curious to explore and open to learn is key in knowing the person, the illness, which is a social response to disease, and the disease itself. R.E.D.E. suggests a simple mnemonic V.I.E.W. (for Vital activities, Ideas, Expectations, and Worries) to explore the patient's perspective and tailor education and treatment planning. Vital activities refers to an individual's occupational, interpersonal, and intrapersonal functioning. Questions might include, "How does it disrupt your daily activity?" or "How does it impact your functioning?" or "What made you decide to come in now?" Often people have a sense of what is happening to them. Asking what ideas someone has about his or her symptoms can be valuable in assuring that we have alleviated our patients' concerns. Alternative questions that elicit patient ideas include, "Do you know others who have had similar symptoms?" and "What have others told you they think is going on?" Eliciting patient expectations also provides an important basis for alignment around the nature of a problem and possible solutions. Questions to elicit patient expectations include, "What are you hoping we can do for you today?" or "What outcome do you hope to achieve with treatment?"

Worries are the final aspect of the V.I.E.W. mnemonic and are intended to elicit what worries or frightens the patient most. Asking directly, "What worries you most about it?" can elicit the patient's perspective while also conveying that it is vital information.

Phase III: Engaging the relationship

The last step in relationship building aligns with the education and treatment stage of a patient encounter. Trust, rapport, and a shared understanding of the patient's perspective all work together to set up the patient and clinician for success in Phase III. Research has demonstrated that patient-clinician agreement on the nature of a problem increases the likelihood of problem resolution.[44] Having experienced success as a partner in his or her visit, a patient feels more motivated and confident in his or her capacity to learn health-related information and collaborate in making decisions and developing a realistic treatment plan. Relationship engagement enhances health outcomes by improving patient comprehension and recall,[45] capacity to give informed consent,[46] patient self-efficacy,[47] treatment adherence, and self-management of chronic illness.[48] Employing a more doctor-centered approach may feel easier and simpler in many ways, but it significantly impedes patient motivation and confidence to engage in behavior change and health maintenance that would otherwise lead to improved health outcomes.[49]

Share diagnosis and information. Telling a patient the medical facts and what he or she needs to know is not sufficient for effective care. We must also be sure that the patient understands the information, which can only be assessed by asking. "What would you like to know about Y?" or "It would help me to know what you know about X." Framing information in the context of the patient's perspective and engaging in dialogue that allows the patient to register new information and ask clarifying questions facilitates patient understanding.[50] It can be helpful to ask patients to reflect back their understanding of information shared. "I want to be sure that I'm explaining things clearly . . ." or "I've given you a lot of information . . ." are helpful ways to preface a request for patients to tell us what they've heard and understood.

Collaboratively develop a plan. Relationship engagement is designed to support patient understanding, decision making, and consideration of potential treatment barriers, such as financial difficulties or limited support. Treatment adherence and behavior change are more likely when the patient is an integral part of the planning process and agrees with the recommendations.[51]

It is the patient's responsibility to make an informed decision about how to proceed, if at all. To do so, it is important to describe the treatment goals and options including risks, benefits, and alternatives. This is when a clinician's experience in diagnosis and treatment planning, as well as knowledge about the efficacy of various treatment options, is of major value to the patient. Sometimes we can have strong convictions about a particular direction to take. Rather than conveying judgment or imposing our perspective, the patient may ultimately be better served by our seeking to better understand what contributes to his or her preference. For instance, "Help me understand what makes this the best option for you." This may facilitate compromise or further negotiation. Other times, you may agree to disagree, but at least you'll have a better understanding of why the patient feels the way he or she does. Once you have a plan, checking for comprehension and any potential barriers to the plan helps to solidify recall, understanding, and adherence.[52]

Provide closure. Ending a visit can easily be taken for granted. However, reviewing the time spent and demonstrating respect and appreciation for the patient provides closure and also engenders continued partnership. Often a misassumption is made that the patient knows when a visit is ending and what to do next. However, it is necessary to alert the patient when a visit is ending and affirm his or her contributions and collaboration. For instance, "We're about out of time. I'm glad you came in today and appreciate your willingness to share what you've been going through. It helps me get a better sense of what's going on and for us to work together to address it." Providing a handshake and personal goodbye along with next steps continues to help the patient navigate his or her medical visit with ease.

Dialogue throughout. Patients are unable to comprehend and accurately recall most of the information presented during a typical medical visit.[53] In our experience, shared decision making can be the most challenging for clinicians because we've created nice, informative monologues on X, Y, and Z. Specialists and primary care physicians alike typically have a three- to five-minute educational monologue about a disease, and don't pause to check whether the patient wants or needs all the information provided. This can be a time sink for clinicians and is easily avoidable with A.R.I.A., a mnemonic representing a sequence for engaging in dialogue throughout the education and treatment stage of a patient visit. A.R.I.A. stands for Assess, Reflect, Inform, Assess (see Figure 4.1). Dialogue as opposed to a monologue keeps the patient involved in the learning process[54] and can improve understanding and recollection.

Power Points

1. Change the goal of communication skills training to develop meaningful relationships with patients. Relationships have the power to heal.

2. By using relationship-centered rather than purely patient-centered communication, your program values and honors the expertise of all stakeholders.

3. Consistently model relationship-centered communication to reinforce a parallel process: the skills required to facilitate participants and the skills we are advocating for with patients are the same.

4. Implement reflective competence as a learning goal to have clinicians actively reflect on why they say what they say.

Chapter 5

Making Communication Skills Resonate with Experienced Clinicians

M otivating physicians to attend and actively engage in communication skills training is often perceived as an enormous feat. We knew if we put a program in front of experienced clinicians, it had to be rock solid. In addition, we wanted to provide participants with an experience equivalent to, if not exceeding, that of a patient. This strategy entailed modeling the skills we teach with one another and with participants in an authentic and meaningful way, recognizing their expertise and valuing their contributions.

Basic Principles of Engagement

We were mindful of Maslow's hierarchy of needs in creating a climate conducive to learning. Maslow proposed that certain needs (biological/physiological, safety, belongingness/love, and esteem) be met in order to reach self-actualization or a state of personal growth and fulfillment.[1] We considered many of Maslow's hierarchy of needs to be absolute prerequisites for an optimal learning environment. Before participants attended the course, they received a detailed e-mail outlining the course, the location, where to park, the number of breaks, meals, and even suggesting a comfortable, layered type of dress to accommodate fluctuating temperatures. If participants had specific requests, such as dietary needs, they were invited to contact our program manager who addressed each and every request. Upon arrival, participants were greeted warmly with a smile and handshake. Rather than rushing into the course content, participants were invited to hang up their coats, get comfortable, and have breakfast.

We also thought about the size of the group and how this would impact learning, safety, connection, and active participation.[2] Groups were maxed at 12 with two facilitators and divided into two smaller groups for skills practice. Groups larger than this can make it easy for some participants to fade into the background, allowing others to dominate the conversation and focus the learning in personal areas of interest that might not be the consensus of the group at large.

To foster a sense of connection and belonging, facilitators were mindful to connect with participants and/or connect participants with each other in a personal manner. Each of these steps was also included to convey value and respect, an important ingredient in establishing a personal relationship and a relationship as part of the group.[3] For those of us facilitating, it was really important to provide colleagues who are hardworking experts in their fields, working under incredible time and task pressure, with an experience that rejuvenated the clinician while improving patient care.

As with any educational intervention, designing a curriculum that can meet all learners "where they are" is a rigorous and critical process. I will highlight the core principles and methods that have made communication skills training effective for our experienced, and sometimes reluctant, learners. Of course, we could not learn what strategies worked without also stumbling upon a few that did not.

Creating Solid Curriculum Grounded in Learning Objectives and Measurement

In his taxonomy of learning,[4] Benjamin Bloom originally identified three domains of learning: knowledge, attitudes, and skills. He proposed that each domain must be mastered prior to proceeding to the next. Nowadays, these domains are often identified as the goals of learning. In curriculum design, it is important to identify what you want to change. In our course, we wanted to focus primarily on the acquisition of specific communication skills, such as collaboratively setting an agenda. However, we also included empirical research to challenge participants' preconceived notions about communication and provide a rationale for change. Clinicians may identify, and certainly respect, a well-designed curriculum that is grounded in educational theory, and strong curricular design gives them another reason to engage fully. We wanted a solid design that would motivate all staff to engage and participate."

In 1959, Donald Kirkpatrick developed and revised a process for evaluating training programs that incorporated Bloom's taxonomy and continues to be widely used today.[5] The process consists of four levels of assessing (1) participant reaction to the program; (2) the specific learning of knowledge, attitudes, or skills; (3) comparison of actual performance before and after the program; and (4) outcomes that result from the integration of newly learned knowledge, attitudes, or skills. We found it helpful to identify specific goals and hypothetically answer Kirkpatrick's questions when designing the curriculum. From there, we sought empirically validated methods whenever possible to increase the likelihood of a positive learning outcome. We also designed pre-, post-, and three-months post surveys to assess each level qualitatively and quantitatively. No matter how much rationale is provided during the pilot phase, a program is only as strong as its evaluation. If we weren't achieving the results we anticipated, we were determined to revamp it until we did.

Engaging Physicians: "What's in It for Me?"

Malcolm Knowles's theory of andragogy, or adult education, posits that for adults to learn new skills, the skills need to be relevant to their personal or professional goals.[6] When choosing continuing education courses, people select courses that appeal to them—a topic relevant to "what I do" or "my specialty," with the hope that it might provide some "knowledge or skill helpful to my practice" and "that I could implement relatively easily." Not only must the skills be useful, they must be feasible to implement. This is certainly true of staff physicians. Coincidentally, the timing of transparency of communication scores created a real need for providers to seek out resources to improve their communication with patients. Once at the course, we worked to foster more internal motivation by appealing to participants' desire to improve patient outcomes and become more efficient, effective, and satisfied with their jobs. Who wouldn't want that?

> *People are more engaged and more interested in what has perceived meaning or value to them.*

Andragogic theory also asserts that adults are more receptive and tend to learn more when education is self-directed or learner-centered.[7] It's worth noting that learner-centeredness also includes respecting the decision of a participant not to learn. We recognized that if we tried to sell clinicians on participating, we might increase resistance to practicing the skills. There were only two occasions during our training of thousands of physicians internally in which individuals had to be pulled outside of the room for a discussion about their decision not to learn. Even then, their perspectives were explored and their behavior addressed because it was disruptive to others' learning efforts. In one case, the learner recognized that he was being disruptive and that this was due primarily to "antibodies" he had developed to prior training. He sent a note of apology after the course, which demonstrated more reflection than one might have typically given him credit for:

> Thanks for all the time you both put into this. I hope I was not the "participant from hell" for you. I did enjoy the conference and did benefit from it. I think all Docs think they are doing a better job of communicating than they really are.

In the other case, the participant made comments about how the course was "stupid" and that he was being "picked on." Recognizing his discomfort, the facilitator pulled him aside, explored his perspective, and highlighted that the course was about the group learning, not his individual behavior. The participant was invited to leave, but he chose to stay. In the end, his take-home word for the day was *empathy*. He mentioned that he had had a tough week prior and he hoped these skills could help in the future. Maintaining appropriate boundaries while modeling empathy and curiosity applies equally to facilitation and clinical work and is just as critical.

The use of reflective listening and empathy were additional skills that facilitators employed to foster self-discovery and insight among participants. Facilitators were invited to share any initial reservations they experienced when learning the skills for the first time. This self-disclosure was usually followed by personal testimony of how the skill was found to be quite helpful later and, in effect, legitimized learners who were grappling with new concepts.

Miller and Rollnick, who developed motivational interviewing as a powerful intervention for behavior change, recommend another technique called *rolling with resistance*.[8] Sometimes this includes acknowledgment or validation statements, such as, "Sounds like a lot of people feel that getting the patient perspective takes time" or "I've felt the same way at times. It can be frustrating to feel you are doing your best, but it still isn't enough." Yet another response we used was to elicit input from other participants by asking, "How many others feel that way?" Such a question encourages dialogue and self-discovery rather than spoon-feeding a particular answer.

We were not always successful in our attempts to avoid defense of the skills. One skill in particular was phrased in such a way as to leave very little room for alternative perspectives: *Elicit all patient concerns early in the visit by using, "What else?"* It was also the one skill most participants criticized. Generally, the criticism was that use of the phrase "What else?" sounded too disingenuous. Often as novice facilitators, we would respond to such criticism by arguing that there was literature that found "What else?" to be more effective than "Anything else?" We'd expound upon the multitude of videotaped encounters that the researchers had reviewed documenting a tendency for the interviewer to shake his or her head yes or no when asking, "Anything else?" that did not occur when asking, "What else?"[9] With such an eloquent explanation, how could learners not agree that we were right and they were wrong? When put that way, we easily recognized that we'd fallen into the all-too-common trap of becoming more teacher-centered than learner-centered. Now not only do we acknowledge and validate participants who criticize this skill, we also have modified the skill to *Ask patient to list all concerns for the visit or hospital stay up front.* If participants are interested in different ways of achieving this skill, and the group is unable to come up with any ideas on their own, we are happy to outline the options including "Is there anything else?" "What else?" and even "Are there some other concerns you'd like to be sure we address?" Only after outlining all the options might we gently weigh in on what has been shown in a few studies. Often, our input isn't necessary. This strategy has worked well to preserve the autonomy of each learner.

> *If we have to prioritize our goals for the day, it is to value their perspective rather than prove how correct we are.*

Reflective Competence and Experiential Learning

Most are familiar with the old adage that practice makes perfect. Still, we need only turn to our professional sports icons that have not one, but multiple coaches to suggest that feedback can be helpful no matter how expert or experienced we may become.[10] Months and certainly years of practice can result in the formation of habits that allow physicians to communicate instinctively, focusing their attention instead on the more imminent needs of the patient. When physicians struggle to identify why they are performing a specific skill, this is aptly termed *unconscious competence*. Unfortunately, performing at an unconsciously competent level can also result in regression of skill or honing of less-than-perfect skills. *Reflective competence*, on the other hand, is character-ized by the ability to be mindful of what, how, and why you are communicating in a particular way. Such awareness and reflection allow us to evaluate and refine our communication in an ongoing manner. It also enables us to tailor our com-munication to each patient, create opportunities to develop innovative communication techniques, and better share the skills with others. It is a vital component in achieving peak performance. Reflective competence resonates with clinicians who often feel belittled by being asked to simply remember a mnemonic or smile more in communication skills training. These efforts, albeit well intentioned, don't honor how difficult communicating effectively can actually be. In a way, reflective competence gives physicians permission to use their clinical judgment and armamentarium of evidence-based skills to decide what language is needed when and where. And for most clinicians, having that control and deference to their expertise can go a long way.

The dominant medical education theory proposes a stepwise progression from unconscious incompetence to conscious incompetence, conscious competence, and finally, unconscious competence.[11] However, Will Taylor proposed that these stages might better be conceptualized as a series of overlapping circles that allow learners to cycle from one stage to the next and back again throughout life (Figure 5.1).[12]

Such a spiral perspective on medical education normal-izes and validates the concept of lifelong learning. By asking clinicians to move from unconscious to reflective competence, we are implicitly affirming their already high level of com-munication skill. Especially for those who expressed a high

FIGURE 5.1 **Medical Education Learning Spiral**

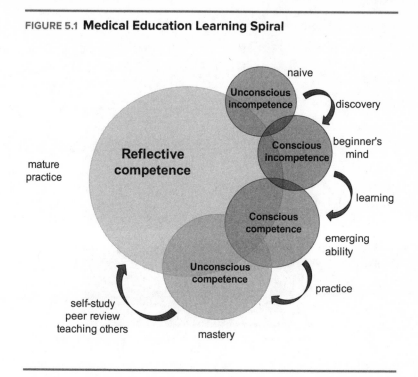

level of confidence in their communication prior to taking our course, we encourage a focus on the collective experience of all the staff and caregivers, and their pivotal role in modeling the skills for the purpose of being able to teach them to others. This is enormously important because only when you recognize that you have something to learn will you be interested in programs that have something to teach.

The Johari window is a concept developed by psychologists Joseph Luft and Harry Ingham to improve personal development and self-awareness. The Johari window also illustrates the fact that what is known by oneself is more limited than that which can be made known by others.[13] Note the practice and learning interventions that transition a learner from one phase to the next in Figures 5.1 and 5.2.

FIGURE 5.2 **The Johari Window**

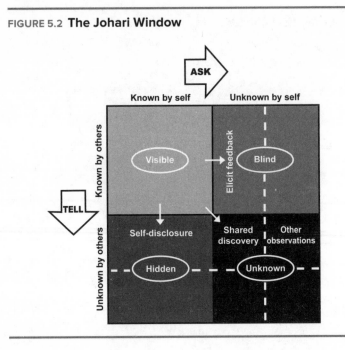

Actively participating in the communication training through observing colleagues' skills practice, exchanging stories, and having a dialogue about skills creates a third opportunity for shared discovery of that which was previously unknown to you or to those around you. The original exercise of the window asked people to choose from a list of adjectives what they thought best described themselves, and then asked the same question of people they knew well. The adjectives were then grouped into these four quadrants.

> *We all have blind spots with respect to how we communicate, and we have to stay curious enough to learn what they are.*

Lessons Learned

Early on, we often heard comments like, "I've practiced for over 20 years. What exactly do you think you can teach me?" and "Regardless of what you may say, of course this is about HCAHPS." Once we removed the slide about HCAHPS, discussing HCAHPS scores became the exception to the rule. Instead of focusing on what the course *was not*, we shifted our focus to what the course objective *was*. In so doing, facilitators were able to speak from a place of passion and authenticity as opposed to the fear they often experienced when trying to convince colleagues that it wasn't about the HCAHPS survey.[14]

The use of standardized patients (SPs) was another opportunity for us to be reminded that what may enhance learning for some might disrupt learning for others. When we developed the course, we decided to use SPs to reduce the artificiality of skills practice in the second and third phases of R.E.D.E. We asked participants to practice Phase I skills with a colleague playing the patient role to establish a degree of safety within each group and familiarity with the feedback process. Then, for Phases II and III, SPs presented for the small group skills practice. We developed a standardized case that we thought most clinicians would be comfortable with and were careful to craft interviewer instructions to provide sufficient context and direction for developing a treatment plan with the patient (Figure 5.3).

The patient was Mrs. Sandy Dilhum, a middle-aged woman presenting for follow-up after having had a heart attack while out of town with her daughters. There is no doubt that participants took their clinician role more seriously when SPs entered the room. After an initial introduction of the concept of SPs, we asked everyone to refer to them only as patients for the rest of the day. After the interview was complete and the interviewer had reflected on his or her practice, the facilitator

FIGURE 5.3 **Phase II Skills Practice: Patient Encounter Form**

Patient Name: Dilhum, Sandy   **Title:** Mrs.
Patient Number: 1234 5678

APPOINTMENT INFORMATION
Visit Type: New   **Physician:** Dr. You
Time of Visit: 11:30 am   **Department:** General Internal Medicine

PATIENT INFORMATION
DOB: 9/30/1962   **Sex:** Female
Address: 685 Drummond Rd.   **City:** Shaker Heights
State: OH   **Zip:** 44120
Home Phone: 123-465-7899   **Marital Status:** Married

APPOINTMENT NOTES:
- Patient is a part-time art teacher, wife, and mother of two daughters, age 12 and 14. She suffered a heart attack while out of town for her daughter's dance competition.
- She was taken to the nearest hospital and had an angioplasty and stent.
- She was started on Plavix (an anti-platelet agent) and Lipitor and asked to follow up with you to continue monitoring her blood pressure and cholesterol.
- Indicate the encounter, elicit the patient's perspective, and continue to provide empathy when the opportunity arises.

Patient Name: Dilhum, Sandy   **Title:** Mrs.
Patient Number: 1234 5678

APPOINTMENT INFORMATION
Visit Type: New   **Physician:** Dr. You
Time of Visit: 11:30 am   **Department:** General Internal Medicine

PATIENT INFORMATION
DOB: 9/30/1962   **Sex:** Female
Address: 685 Drummond Rd.   **City:** Shaker Heights
State: OH   **Zip:** 44120
Home Phone: 123-465-7899   **Marital Status:** Married

APPOINTMENT NOTES:
- ***This is a continuation of the same-day visit you had with Mrs. Dilhum during Phase II. Tests revealed the heart attack to be a single lesion/single vessel disease with low risk of future events. Family history is positive for high blood pressure, high cholesterol, and coronary artery disease. She was started on Plavix (an anti-platelet agent) and Lipitor.
- Begin by sharing the test results/diagnosis with your patient. Provide education as appropriate, and negotiate a plan before ending the interview. Remember to partner with the patient and frame the diagnosis and plan in terms of the patient's concerns as much as possible.
- Possible options for the plan include: 1. Continued medication management (Plavix and Lipitor)
     2. Ongoing monitoring of her blood pressure and cholesterol
     3. Exercise regimen

would ask, "How did you feel, Mrs. Dilhum?" SPs were trained to respond only to how they felt and what they appreciated or would have preferred in a visit. We also realized early on that many clinicians have become so specialized that they are very uncomfortable with cases that fall outside their particular specialty. They easily became anxious about not knowing anything about that particular diagnosis or what questions they should be asking. Even when directed not to focus on the medical facts, they struggled to untrain their brains. To address this, facilitators and standardized patients tailored the Dilhum case to an individual's specialty. For example, if a participant's specialty was dermatology, we'd adapt the case so that Mrs. Dilhum was presenting for a rash that she suspects is associated with medication she started following her recent heart attack. Guidelines were developed around how best to adapt the case so that standardized patients felt comfortable with these last-minute changes. These changes put the focus back on the communication skill, not solving the medical case.

Ultimately, we reevaluated the use of SPs when we began training advanced care providers (ACPs). Within one class, we might have a speech pathologist, a nurse practitioner, a general bedside nurse, an administrator, and a social worker. Crafting a case that was adaptable to all of these disciplines was time-consuming, challenging, and often resulted in more anxiety for participants. Recognizing the importance of balancing task competency and task difficulty to maintain participants' learning edge, we decided to remove this added complication to the skills practice. We piloted advanced care provider courses without SP cases. This pilot was met with significantly reduced anxiety from participants and facilitators and eventually was rolled out to the physician courses as well. Given that there are usually costs associated with using SPs, balancing where and when they have the most impact is worth considering.

Facilitating an integrative skills practice presented a third learning opportunity. After didactic, demonstration, and skill practice sessions for each phase of R.E.D.E., we asked everyone in the group to share a specific case they'd encountered that posed a communication challenge. From those, one or two cases were selected by the group to practice. While this allowed for an opportunity to apply all the R.E.D.E. skills in one encounter and often rejuvenated the group's energy, it was not without its challenges. First and foremost, facilitators were facing what felt like the most challenging part of their facilitation at the end of the day. Many also did not feel confident in their ability to facilitate the integrative skills practice effectively. When facilitators were asked what they wanted to work on in faculty development, facilitation of the integrative skills practice was repeatedly the response. In addition, there was an ever-present risk of getting bogged down in the minutiae of the case itself. For instance, if the communication challenge pertained to a patient who was angry about being rejected for a surgical procedure, the group might become focused on the ethics or technicalities of surgical evaluation. Or the group might ask the participant who proposed the case to explain the reasoning behind a particular decision. Not only did this result in conversation irrelevant to communication skills practice, it also posed the risk of an unsafe atmosphere in which others less familiar with the case might cast judgment on the clinicians's medical decisions. Needless to say, facilitating the integrative cases felt like navigating dangerous terrain.

The solution came in the form of action methods and completely redefined our notion of active learning. The distinction between active and passive learning is often characterized by the degree to which learners are able to direct their own learning. For instance, in passive learning, students are viewed as empty vessels in need of filling. Active learning, on the other hand, recognizes the ability of learners to ask questions and generate possible answers. Originally derived from sociodrama and psychodrama, action methods refer to a set of techniques that allows a group of learners to engage mind and body in examining interpersonal conflict along with potential resolution or management strategies and skills. The first step is warming up participants through the use of exercises that reduce participant anxiety and increase their openness to being spontaneous and honest with one another. Warm-ups are most effective when designed to move from fun and lighthearted to focus on the more serious and yet transparent issues that participants may be facing. For instance, when we were first learning action methods, we all met on a weekend, so one of the warm-ups consisted of asking participants to stand in various parts of the room that represented what we were giving up to be there (e.g., family time, exercise, other work obligations, etc.). We were able to recognize the commitment that everyone made to being there on a weekend to learn new facilitation tools, and this helped us to move past it and get down to business.

The second step is similar to the more traditional integrative case method in which we elicited a challenging communication from each participant. However, instead of summarizing the details of each scenario, we only summarized the specific communication challenge (e.g., breaking bad news, managing mismatched expectations). Participants then vote to achieve group consensus on the one case they want to practice. The third step entails development of a new case around the agreed-upon challenge by *interviewing for role*. Interviewing for role requires participants to take turns suggesting the characteristics of the patient and provider. This alone has proven energizing and therapeutic as participants recognize common themes and acknowledge the complexity that patients often present with. *Doubling*, or asking participants to share from the patient or clinician's perspective feelings they might be experiencing but are too professional to say, is another strategy used to help participants better understand the perspectives of both parties. In one case involving narcotic-seeking behaviors, doubling was applied to the physician as well, which creatively highlights to everyone the depth and range of emotions and impact our patients can have on us. The method ensures that the clinician is also *seen*. To best ensure the success of the learner in the designated hot seat, a fourth step involves asking the group to brainstorm strategies or skills that might assist in resolving the conflict. The skills practice is started, and the facilitator continues to look for opportunities in which one party or the other may not be responding from a place of genuine empathy, interest, or curiosity. When this occurs, doubling or other techniques can be further employed to deepen understanding. A fifth and final step is debriefing the skills practice by appreciating the participants, shaking off the roles, and eliciting learning points.

Not only did facilitators demonstrate greater confidence in having a step-by-step process to follow, but also in seeing the energy and enthusiasm from start to finish with action methods. Participants commonly shared aha moments stemming from speaking as the patient or provider in doubling or watching a particular communication skill work effectively. Thus, action methods engaged facilitators and learners in a powerful way to explore and develop skills collaboratively to address challenging communication scenarios in the healthcare setting.

Sustaining Facilitator Engagement

Relationships require tending. Facilitators taught once a month to maintain their facilitation skill set and contribute to maintaining good access for participants. However, midway through the mandated rollout, facilitators were often teaching three or more times a month to meet the high volume of participants. This created a new challenge of facilitator fatigue. We employed a number of strategies to minimize facilitator fatigue. First, we continued to refine the curriculum based on facilitator contributions so that they had ownership of the course while continuously improving it. We worked hard to balance our desire for a standardized course and method with facilitators' needs to be authentic and creative and to apply their personal styles. Second, facilitators needed protected time. Often a call or letter from leadership was sufficient, but when we were asked to roll out the course to all physicians, it became necessary to buy out facilitators' time.

Furthermore, we found that giving presentations locally and nationally about the work we were doing served to renew feelings of purpose and meaning in facilitating the course. The skills taught are empirically validated and work! We encouraged facilitators to speak within their specialty audience about their skills and the subsequent impact on their clinical and professional efficacy. In addition, our homegrown Train the Trainer program was recognized for its value in training prospective leaders. This recognition resulted in facilitators being offered additional professional growth opportunities in and out of the center (e.g., advanced peer coaching, professionalism initiatives, etc.).

Ongoing faculty development was held quarterly, and social engagements for group relationship formation and ongoing development were key to sustaining the engagement of facilitators. We were always looking to add new facilitation tools to their toolbox. One facilitator described these activities as an oasis that she hoped we would preserve forever.

Power Points

1. Attend to the basic needs of your participants to convey value and respect, which can foster an openness to learn.

2. You don't have to be an expert in educational theory, but ground your program in its key components so your curriculum is solid.

3. HCAHPS doesn't inspire most clinicians, so leave it out of the discussion.

4. If something isn't working or is too costly, such as SPs, work around it.

5. Use action methods, which are highly effective means of engaging participants in unexpected ways.

6. Plan from the outset how you will continue facilitator engagement and skill development.

Conversations That Haunt Clinicians

I still have nightmares.

—CARDIAC SURGEON REFLECTING ON BEING
AN INTERN DECADES EARLIER AND TELLING
A FAMILY THEIR LOVED ONE HAD DIED

(Vicente J. Velez) stood outside the door of a family meeting room, hesitating to knock. Inside waited the wife and the mother of John, a patient who was admitted yet again to the hospital for pneumonia and respiratory distress. For years, John had suffered a rare and cruel neurodegenerative disorder that slowly but surely robbed him of his youth, vitality, and spirit. He was known and loved by many. He was a husband, a father, a son, and a friend. I stood there like I had many times before. This time, though, something about the scenario hit too close to home. I stood frozen, paralyzed by fear and sorrow; it was my job to deliver the news that John might have only a few months left to live. It would be necessary to facilitate a discussion about planning the last days of his life. The medical team knew that this was not a discussion that the family was ready to have. During past encounters, they had refused to believe he would die from this disorder.

Empathy is a hardwired trait. When other individuals suffer, we can imagine what it might be like to be in that person's shoes and our brains actually register the feeling. This capacity likely facilitated the growth of civil, structured societies based on justice, the common good, and shared goals. In some sense, we evolved to have the pain of an individual become the pain of the tribe. Medical training could not completely numb a very real neural mechanism that took millions of years to develop.[1] In the case of John, I saw myself in him. Death can come to anyone at a moment's notice. There was an undeniable possibility that one day I could very well leave my wife a widow at a young age, have my parents endure the agony of burying their child, and never give my young child the opportunity to play a game of catch with Dad.

On that winter afternoon many years ago, I had to deliver news that would bring pain I would not wish on anyone. As I was in the midst of fulfilling this unwelcome responsibility, John's family members, in deep pain that turned into rage, blamed me—for not having a cure, for not trying hard enough, for abandoning them at their darkest hour, and for his impending death. It was an afternoon that stays with me to this day.

> *Medical practice is a minefield of encounters that haunt clinicians.*[2]

Doctors in popular culture have consistently been portrayed as poised, objective, and heroic,[3] yet the reality is that they, too, suffer as a result of the care they provide.[4] Moments like these can haunt them for a lifetime. When we don that immaculate white coat, we take on the expectation of being all-knowing and brilliant.[5] We also personify hope, safety, predictability, and goodwill.[6] Yet in reality, clinicians feel pain, resentment, conflict aversion, fear, vulnerability, and inadequacy.[7] The white coat actually may represent a defense for us, our shield against people knowing that we have feelings and don't always have the answers.

Each of us brings our own stories and feelings to the patient encounter, and we also know that aspects of particular patient-clinician relationships often shape such feelings. The most challenging encounters involve demands for unnecessary or inappropriate treatment, patients who are unsatisfied with their care, and unrealistic expectations. Physicians report that one in six patient encounters is difficult.[8] Physicians often find such encounters time-consuming and professionally dissatisfying and secretly hope that these patients will not return.[9] Doctors reporting high numbers of difficult cases were more likely to be young and to feel burned out.[10]

> *Difficult encounters become more stressful if clinicians fail to separate "what we do" from "who we are."*

If "what we do" results in a patient's negative outcome, lack of happiness, or lack of cooperation and we equate our job with our identity, this can adversely affect us at our core, no matter how confident we appear in our white coat.

Medicine ranks among the most stressful occupations. Depression, disengagement, and professional burnout are harsh realities of the profession.[11] Four hundred physicians committed suicide in 2013.[12] Reflecting on the cases that haunt us can help us understand burnout. Being deeply invested in the care that we provide, feeling inadequate when tough conversations arise, and lacking a safe space to talk it through is a recipe for burnout. Here's the big secret about haunting conversations: challenging communication scenarios haunt clinicians because the clinician feels like a failure. They experience shame, helplessness, and guilt. If someone is angry, lashing out at them, or crying uncontrollably, it must be their fault. They must have done something wrong, right? Of course not. These reactions are not about the clinician, but it is the clinician who bears the responsibility, the clinician who carries the emotional weight of his or her own feelings, as well as those of the patient and loved ones.

Relationships are therapeutic. Effective relationship-building skills can be leveraged not only to motivate and inspire patients to take an active role in their own health, but also to help weather the difficult parts that can haunt either party. What can the medical community learn from this? How can we establish and maintain functional, effective, and meaningful relationships with patients when things don't go according to the script?

I will explore key principles in tough scenarios, the cases that haunt us, and insights into how to approach them.

Key Principles

In our skills practice, we initially chose a challenging case based on a real patient and then had the clinician involved in the case play the patient. Unfortunately, this format often tapped into their defenses as the clinician in the case. We would often see the physician become increasingly adamant about how difficult the patient was. By making the patient impossible and unresponsive to any approach, the clinician would demonstrate that the challenge was entirely the patient's fault, not because the clinician had used ineffective strategies. At times, it felt as if we were dance instructors who had students whose goal was to prove that dancing was impossible. It isn't the purpose of the exercise—although it might be therapeutic for the clinician to be seen and heard— to show colleagues "see what I'm up against." But we risk losing the rest of the group if they do not feel any ownership of the case being simulated.

So we decided to have the group build a case rather than use a specific case supplied by one of the participants. We had each participant present a type of case he or she found challenging rather than a specific one. We listed the challenges and had the participants vote on which theme they wanted to practice. The group then built a specific case around that theme, and everyone contributed details about the case. This pivotal change not only encouraged group ownership of the case, but also avoided triggering the painful memories of a single participant.

"Taking Care of the Hateful Patient" was a seminal article in the *New England Journal of Medicine*.[13] It had broad appeal to physicians because it validated how difficult it can be to care for some patients—but it labeled patients as "dependent clingers," "entitled demanders," and other negative monikers. We avoided this at all costs. If physicians are accepting of patients being labeled, then we'd better be comfortable being labeled, too! It felt like the wrong direction for this work.

> The idea of relationship-centered care is to understand the goals, drivers, and perspectives of those we serve, not to label them because it makes us feel better.

This labeling also implies that patients are the problem, and effectively shifts the locus of control away from us and anything we could possibly say or do.

Given how sensitive this work can be for clinicians, they must be handled with care. The facilitator must be acutely aware of the sweet spots for maximal learning and avoid triggering deeply painful memories that may derail learning. Empathic curiosity is necessary to help participants feel supported before even approaching these conversations. Here are a few V.I.E.W. questions adapted for participants:

What does your professional world look like?

What are your common communication challenges, and how do they make you feel?

How do challenging encounters affect you?

What would be most helpful for you?

What have you tried?

What are your ideas about what will be effective here?

What obstacles do you see to improving communication in this scenario?

In the past, have we taught clinicians how to say no to patients demanding inappropriate treatment while also making sure these patients have a good experience? Have we also taught clinicians how to tell family members that their loved one has died without feeling at fault? And in cases where it was their fault, how have we supported clinicians? We haven't. We have acted as if these realities didn't exist, and we have badgered clinicians about their HCAHPS scores. No wonder they have felt disengaged and isolated. We have an enormous opportunity to honor the sacredness of this work if we choose to. It's a pivotal opportunity.

TABLE 6.1 **Most Common Communication Scenarios that Haunt Clinicians**

Theme	Typical Reported Example
Chronic pain in setting of opiate use or abuse	Patient demanding opiates early, by specific type and/or dose in emergency room or from a covering provider
Unrealistic expectations	Patient thinks that a fourth redo back surgery will fix her lower back pain and came to you because you are the best doc
Strong emotion, usually as a result of bad news	After being given a cancer diagnosis, the patient or family becomes angry and lashes out at the clinician
Multiple symptoms without cohesive medical diagnosis (somatoform disorders)	Patient presents with a thick, color-coded binder of symptoms and believes that his symptoms are related to mold exposure

Notes and Excerpts from the R.E.D.E. Practice Sessions

Cases that participants identify as difficult communication scenarios fall into common categories (Table 6.1).

Case 1: Chronic pain

The patient is a 40-year-old man who was injured in a motor vehicle accident six years ago. Since then, he has continually suffered from severe back, leg, and rib pain at the sites of injury. He has been on the oral opioid oxycodone 5 mg as needed every eight hours for pain. He is here for his follow-up visit one week earlier than scheduled because he was recently hospitalized. He shows up at your clinic rating pain at an "11 out of 10" and asking for resumption of opioid prescriptions, with an additional request for increased dosage and frequency.

The dilemma for the caregiver here is balancing the need to provide sound medical care with the impulse to relieve suffering. The clinician's experience may be that denying a patient pain relief with a quick opioid fix is cruel and uncomfortable, or the practitioner may feel so manipulated that he or she becomes angry. A typical dialogue might fail to set boundaries, avoid discussion of areas of conflict, or involve stonewalling, simply giving in, or agreeing to an inappropriate compromise. Any of these can result in enabling the same vicious cycle that will invariably perpetuate or worsen the pain condition or even lead to a fatal overdose or complication such as respiratory failure. Despite the fact that patients suffering from chronic pain and opioid dependency generate strong feelings in providers, there is no reason a chronic pain patient should be denied the opportunity to form an authentic relationship with a healthcare provider, one that includes rapport and an exploration of the patient's concerns, agenda, and perspective. Unfortunately, the clinician's own reaction to these patients or the stigmatization of this group of patients can prevent the practitioner from responding with empathy.

Strategies to practice: Understanding and acknowledging that chronic pain is an incurable condition represents a key first step that has to be the foundation of any honest conversation. The goal for management strategies is to improve quality of life, function, and coping skills in the patient without compromising the patient's health, well-being, and safety. Pain symptoms and the quest for more tests and procedures should be deemphasized. Psychological wounds and damage often perpetuate chronic pain, and avenues to address these wounds should be provided. Given that these are the goals in mind, how do we get there? What words and actions are effective?

Effective statements that we have heard from our physician participants are:

"Help me understand how the pain affects you." (explore impact)

"It must be hard to feel judged." (emotion naming)

"I wish to be honest about what we can do." "I wish there was a quick fix here, but there just isn't." ("I wish" statements)[14]

"This is also frustrating for me as someone who wants to see you feeling better." (limited self-disclosure)

Key elements include determining the patient's agenda, eliciting the patient's narrative of his or her illness, and using empathy to demonstrate a genuine interest in and concern for the patient's experience and suffering. The S.A.V.E. mnemonic also provides some possibilities:

S: Support—"I am here to work on this pain with you."

A: Acknowledge—"Chronic pain is a terrible thing to live with. It's a credit to you that you have been working hard to maintain a job and keep your life together."

V: Validate—"I think anyone who has struggled with pain for as long as you have might feel the same way."

E: Emotion naming—"You really seem incredibly frustrated."

Another helpful acronym is V.I.E.W.:

V: Vital activities—"Tell me more about how this pain has affected you. What has been the impact of using pain medication on the rest of your life? How do others feel about your opioid use?"

I: Ideas—"What are your ideas about how we might manage your pain from here? What benefits do you get from Percocet? What are the downsides to using pain medication for the rest of your life? Other than more Percocet, what are you willing to consider to help your pain?"

E: Expectations—"What are you hoping I can do? Tell me more about your goals."

W: Worries—"What worries you most about your pain and your use of pain medications?"

Setting boundaries does not mean withholding empathy. Setting boundaries is an expression of care and a commitment to having an authentic relationship. As parents, if we refuse to cave in to a child's demand for chocolate cake as a main course for dinner, our standing firm is an expression of concern for our child's well-being. He will be upset because we said no, but he will be better off in the long run eating a healthy diet. The boundary statement should be firm, sure-footed, and followed by silence. Here are a few examples:

"I will not be prescribing the Percocet today. I hope we can work on a different approach."

"I do not think that your continued use of oxycodone is a good idea."

"Opioids are not a good option for you."

When a boundary is set, patients may or may not be at a phase of change where they will accept counseling. Preaching the dangers of opioids does not help. We do not want to engage in a debate about the pros and cons of opioids for chronic pain. Debates have winners and losers—and no one wants to lose. Instead, invite self-discovery from the patient.

The A.R.I.A. (Ask, Reflect, Inform, and Assess) cycle can be an effective tool for this. Using A.R.I.A. in this instance can help assess insight, health literacy, the phase of change the patient is in, the patient's level of interest in change, and ideas and strategies that may help.

Here are some dialogue quotes from skills practice:

DOCTOR: Why do you think I am reluctant to prescribe additional oxycodone? (explore impact)

PATIENT: Maybe you think I am addicted. But I am in real pain, Doc.

DOCTOR: I believe it is real. I want to work together to find a way to get your quality of life back. (validate, partner with patient, focus on goals)

PATIENT: I hope so. Why are you so worried about this, Doc? What's the big deal? Just give me the prescription, and I promise I won't be any trouble.

DOCTOR: I really am worried about your condition and even more so because what we have been doing doesn't seem to be working. I can explain if you are interested. (self-disclosure of worry)

PATIENT: Go ahead.

Case 2: Unrealistic expectations

The patient is a 70-year-old woman who underwent emergency colectomy two months ago for massive hemorrhage from extensive diverticulosis. She is a dialysis patient and has COPD, insulin-dependent diabetes poorly controlled, and a recent massive heart attack. She is on anticoagulation and dual antiplatelet therapy. A cardiologist told

her she was a very high-risk surgical candidate and recommended no surgery, including colostomy reversal. She
is very angry when told that surgery is not advised and
demands that it be done anyway.

There are many variations of this case, wherein a
physician's recommendations do not match the patient's
expectations. When we are uncomfortable in a difficult
conversation, we often default to attempting to persuade
emotional patients by using data. ("You have multiple stents,
and coming off the platelet therapy is dangerous.") We may
well be correct about the medical facts, but overpowering
patients with our superior medical knowledge does not help
our relationship with them. Moreover, when patients are
upset, a cognitive approach generally has no impact, except
for, sometimes, making them more upset. The key learning
here is this: the emotional brain does not respond to data. It
responds to recognition of the emotion.

Strategies to practice: In cases where there is conflict, "competing" with the patient at the point of disagreement is generally
not helpful. In this case, the point of disagreement is whether
or not to go through with colostomy reversal. This argument
could go on forever. What we invite our learners to do is to
address the conflict from the point of the patient's goals (vital
activities), ideas, expectations, and worries (V.I.E.W.). The
next step is to find a way to align with the patient and his or
her goals. If done right, it will not be a conflict between the
practitioner and the patient, but rather a partnership that will
tackle whatever is standing in the way of the patient's goals. If
we assume that neither party wants the patient to die in the
perioperative period and that both parties want to improve
the patient's quality of life, then a partnership with common
goals is possible. The initial medical recommendation may

stand or change, boundaries may have to be set, and the patient may still be unsatisfied. Whatever the outcome, an alignment of perspectives does wonders to help patient and clinician see eye to eye, or at least view a disagreement from a position of mutual respect. Reflective listening, S.A.V.E., V.I.E.W., and A.R.I.A. can all help here.

Here are some dialogue quotes from skills practice sessions:

DOCTOR: It sounds like this surgery was important to you. (reflective listening)

PATIENT: You bet. Now *you ruined my life!*

DOCTOR: I'm sorry (long pause). I do not want to ruin your life. Please help me understand why the operation is so important to you. (empathy with apology, open-ended question to explore impact, state difference between perception and intention)

PATIENT: Prior to that emergency operation, I managed to get by and enjoy my trips to the senior center. My friends and social life at the senior center have given me a reason to live. Now, this colostomy is hideous, it irritates my skin, and it stinks when it leaks. I am embarrassed to be seen in this condition around my friends. I keep to myself now, and I'm much less active. I simply want my life back. I was hoping the reversal would do that.

DOCTOR: Thank you for sharing that. I'm sorry that your colostomy is giving you so much trouble. It sounds like what's important to you and what you miss are the social connections that have been interrupted ever since this happened. (reflective listening)

PATIENT: Right!

DOCTOR: OK, that helps me. Why do you believe we are reluctant to proceed with surgery? (asking for patient ideas, A.R.I.A.)

PATIENT: Well, now that I think about it, I believe you think surgery is too risky since I've had a recent heart attack.

DOCTOR: That's right. I'd hate to see you have major complications or worse from undergoing more surgery. It doesn't help you if you don't survive or if you end up with a worse quality of life because the operation didn't go well. (inform, A.R.I.A.)

PATIENT: I guess.

DOCTOR: Knowing your perspective helps. We can talk further about addressing the issues with the colostomy that concern you the most during these planned trips to the senior center. We can also work on reducing leakage, how to hide it, and managing the skin irritation. (align with goals, depart from point of conflict) How does this sound to you? (assess, A.R.I.A.)

PATIENT: It sounds OK. Thanks for listening.

Case 3: Strong emotion

A 45-year-old man presents to your clinic for follow-up. He came in with weight loss and anemia. Workup shows an aggressive colon cancer. CT scans reveal multiple lesions in the lung and liver, consistent with metastatic disease. The physician reveals, "We have confirmed that you have colon cancer and it has spread to the lungs and liver." The patient, although having come to expect such news, is in utter shock. Silent at first, he responds in rage: "This is your fault! *You should have caught this sooner!* What's going to happen to my wife and kids? I have a death sentence, and you don't care!"

In this case, the physician has delivered devastating news without preparing the patient or assessing his readiness. The patient is shocked and becomes enraged, distraught, and emotionally hijacked. While bad news will sometimes be met with such reactions, there are communication skills that help keep us and our patients aligned. The foundational skills still apply. Keep in mind that many people go through specific stages of grief: anger, denial, bargaining, and acceptance. What is not constant, however, is the length of time it takes to go through all stages.[15]

Strategies to practice: The learning point for giving bad news and responding to the predictable aftermath of strong emotion is to give the patient some control over the flow of information and to utilize what he already knows.[16] We may inform the patient that we have his test results back and inquire whether he wants to review them or if now is a good time. We may ask if there is someone else whom he wishes to be present for support or other reasons. We may remind him what tests were done and ask what he understands the purpose of those tests was. Actively involving the patient in a conversation about what has been done, why, and what it revealed helps keep the patient in an active partnership with the clinician. After bad news is delivered clearly and concisely, we practice silence, and deliver support and empathy. We often see clinicians filling silent spaces with words. This space needs to remain empty for a while. It shouldn't be filled with words born of our own discomfort.

Here are some dialogue quotes from skills practice sessions:

PATIENT: I have a death sentence, and you don't care!

DOCTOR: (silence, gives patient time to break silence)

DOCTOR: I've delivered very painful news. I wish things were different. (emotion naming, "I wish" statement)

PATIENT: (crying)

DOCTOR: (offers tissue or touches shoulder if appropriate, other nonverbal cues that reflect the severity of the moment, such as mirroring body language and expression)

Case 4: Somatoform disorders

Patient is a 35-year-old male from out of town, plagued by years of fatigue, lack of energy, severe headaches, ringing in the ears, and inability to concentrate. He complains of an occasional skin rash that occurs at random times and has taken serial photographs of his skin. He has visited numerous specialists, including outside tertiary centers. He was told that there was "nothing they can do." He comes in with a suitcase full of medical records and is in your office for a second opinion. He believes that there is an underlying systemic illness, possibly parasites, that no one has diagnosed yet. He is desperate for a cure and wishes for some form of exploratory surgery.

Somatoform disorders are a broad category of mental illness that includes somatization, hypochondriasis, Munchausen syndrome, and conversion disorders. Criteria for diagnosis include age, duration of symptoms, and multiple bodily symptoms in the absence of a causative medical diagnosis. The suffering of these patients is real, and most patients, like their doctors, feel very frustrated by the lack of a definitive diagnosis. The thoughts driving the beliefs may be strongly anchored, associated with personality disorders and/or abuse, and not easy to dispel. Thorough and reasonable differential diagnoses should always be considered first, with appropriate evaluations. Interestingly, even though clinicians can identify these patients, we don't always tell them what we think they have.

Strategies to practice: In addition to strategies we have already talked about, deemphasizing the focus on obtaining the correct diagnosis or making the symptoms go away may be helpful. Empathic statements should also be geared less toward the frustration around the diagnostic mystery or the symptoms. For the health professional, this can be challenging to do, because we were trained to figure out what is wrong with a patient. Instead, the leap we need to help the patient make is to focus on functional recovery, with an emphasis on a mutual commitment to focus on agreed-upon functional goals. Accomplishing this goal requires choosing the right words. Telling a patient that "this is all in your head" sounds like a value judgment and will alienate anyone. It also fails to validate the real suffering these patients endure. Instead, we suggest, "Our tests indicate that your hardwiring or anatomy is OK, but the functioning is not" or "What would it mean to you if there isn't a medical diagnosis here?" or "Have you ever considered that the symptoms may be related to stress?"

The most important step is to do no harm. Most harm that afflicts these patients is from us, due to complications from multiple tests, multiple surgeries, or increased anxiety if tests are equivocal. Instead of more testing, establishing and maintaining a trusting relationship can make the difference for these patients. In referring to mental health specialists, it helps to frame the referral as a general way to help with coping. "Given the impact these symptoms have had on your life, I'm wondering if we can support you more effectively. Most people wouldn't be able to cope with all of this."

Here are some dialogue quotes from skills practice sessions:

PATIENT: I need surgery now. I can sometimes feel the parasites crawl all over my skin. I swear some might be in my brain. I need a surgeon to explore my body, get samples.

DOCTOR: I can't even imagine. Tell me how this is affecting your life. (acknowledgment, assessing impact)

PATIENT: I can't concentrate, and I've been fired from work as a marketing specialist for lack of productivity. So what about that surgery? It will help me, right?

DOCTOR: Sounds like you're hoping it will. Well, I looked through your records, and I've talked to other experts. Our tests do not show any structural abnormalities. (reflecting and informing in A.R.I.A.)

PATIENT: I find that hard to believe. I swear something is wrong.

DOCTOR: I know you do not feel well. I want to be honest with you and help you to get your life back. What I can offer is to work with you toward the things we can do to achieve that goal. (reflective listening, "I wish" statement, aligning goals, support in S.A.V.E.)

PATIENT: I do not know what to believe. You're the twenty-fifth doctor I've seen.

If the patient says, "OK, I'll give this a shot," then you can offer the whole treatment plan based on functional recovery, cognitive behavioral therapy, and therapeutic visits while firmly deemphasizing symptoms and determination of diagnosis throughout the relationship.

If the patient says, "No, this is bull. I've had it with all of you doctors. I'm seeking my twenty-sixth opinion," then you can offer continued support should there be a subsequent change of heart: "I'm sorry to hear that. My door remains open if there is any way I can help in the future." In our experience, most clinicians are uncomfortable with this approach, yet we view it as an essential skill. That is, knowing when to end a conversation so it doesn't irrevocably damage the relationship is a skill like any other.

Lessons Learned

These four cases are a glimpse into some of the most common challenging cases for clinicians, this is by no means a comprehensive guide on how to navigate each of them. Other common challenges include interprofessional conflict, various varieties of intense emotion, verbal abuse, disclosing errors, or threats of lawsuits. The themes and approaches for such cases are somewhat similar to those discussed here: attending first and foremost to the relationship is generally the best strategy. In each of these challenging cases lies an opportunity to set aside the medical agenda for a moment and focus on the relationship with the patient. We should ask ourselves, "Who is this human being, and how can I be most helpful?" By focusing on building authentic connections based on genuine interest and caring, we bridge the disconnection, form partnerships, and align toward common goals. We must resist the urge to "fix" emotions and acknowledge our limited ability to fix medical problems.

Perhaps more important, in facilitating challenging scenarios, we've learned that these cases leave a profound impact on the clinician. In the courses, clinicians often say, "I thought I was the only one having these conversations," which speaks to the isolation that exists in real practice. These scenarios leave wounds that often don't have a chance to heal fully. The clinician sees the next patient and has few opportunities to process traumatic encounters. Most clinicians are fiercely committed to doing the right thing for patients. Our hope is that by recognizing that suffering is at the core of the vast majority of challenging communications, clinicians can learn to decrease not only the patient's suffering but also their own.

Power Points

1. Recognize that caring for patients can be difficult and that most clinicians are deeply invested in the care they provide. Because of this, communication that goes poorly can cause tremendous suffering for patients and clinicians alike, suffering that may not have an outlet.

2. Align your facilitation approach to support the clinician and enable the clinician to share these experiences.

3. Be ready. The most haunting conversations fall into predictable buckets: chronic pain with opiate requests, unrealistic expectations, strong emotion from bad news, and somatization disorders.

4. No new models are needed to navigate these conversations. Reinforce foundational skills.

Chapter 7

Individual Peer Coaching

What to Do About Dr. Jones?

"Do you know why we never see my husband's urologist anymore?" A patient's wife asked one day.

"No, tell me."

"After Frank (her husband) had his biopsies done, the urologist called on the phone and I answered. He said to me, 'Would you please do me a favor and tell your husband that he has prostate cancer?'"

The story reminded me of a time when I (Timothy Gilligan) was a fellow and was rounding on the patient of a famous oncologist. The oncologist wasn't with me that day, and the patient asked me, "Where's Dr. Doubt It?"

I was puzzled. "Who is Dr. Doubt It?" I asked. "You know," the patient replied, "Dr. _____," and he named the famous oncologist.

"Why do you call him Dr. Doubt It?" I asked.

"Because," the patient replied, "when I asked him if he thought I'd still be alive in a year, he said, 'I doubt it.'"

And then there was the day my wife, a cardiologist, called very upset because of the way a surgeon had spoken to her. He had asked her to perform a study on a patient to confirm a finding that radiology had reported and that he doubted. It took a couple of hours to get the test done, and it revealed that the radiology report was incorrect and that, therefore, the patient could undergo an operation that had been planned for earlier that morning.

"You f*#@ing f*#@," the surgeon screamed, "Why did it take so f*#@ing long? Now I'm going to be stuck in the f*#@ ing O.R. until midnight!"

In the prior chapter, you read about how difficult caregiving can be for patients in their darkest moments and the impact that can have on clinicians. Sometimes, physicians respond to these challenges by building resilience and effective coping skills. Other times, it brings out the worst in us. One of the challenges we faced teaching a standardized full-day communication skills course was to be responsive to the needs and skill levels of individual clinicians. By making the course highly learner-centered, we could meet the vast majority of learners at a level that was relevant and challenging for them. For some clinicians, however, a full-day course conducted away from the setting in which they practiced was inadequate. With our team leading a new push to train clinicians to communicate more effectively, it was natural that colleagues would ask how we could help with physicians and others who needed more individualized attention. These clinicians were outliers with regard to communication skills or were getting into trouble because of recurrent problems related to interpersonal interactions. What, we were asked, could be done about clinicians who:

- Told a patient sitting on an exam table in her underwear that she was fat
- Antagonized colleagues to the point that they wanted to leave their job
- Treated patients in such a manner that colleagues would no longer refer patients to them because of complaints
- Had multiple patients in a six-month period report that they would refuse to see that clinician ever again
- Got into a shouting argument with a hospitalized patient

For these sorts of individuals and for others who simply wanted more help, we started offering one-on-one coaching. We thought that by providing more sustained and focused attention on individuals, we could intervene in a more effective manner. Moreover, in the sorts of challenges described above, there was typically an unusually large deficit in self-awareness, one that required more sustained attention and work to correct. At the same time, such work was highly labor-intensive and thus could only be offered to a limited number of individuals. In this chapter, we will describe our approach to coaching, which others might describe as a blend of coaching and mentoring.

What Is Coaching?

As noted by Atul Gawande in an essay in the *New Yorker* magazine, it seems strange that, unlike professional athletes and opera singers, physicians do not generally have anyone coaching them to help them improve their performance once their training ends.[1] LeBron James, Tom Brady, and the stars who perform at La Scala are at the top of their fields and yet have coaches helping them maintain and grow their skills.

They aim to continually improve and recognize that they can benefit from help and from working on their skills in the context of a relationship. Why is the same not true of physicians? Although the examples presented at the beginning of this chapter describe situations where remediation was needed, coaching does not imply remediation. Instead, it implies an interest in and commitment to improving. In fact, there are substantial numbers of physicians who have approached us about wanting more personalized coaching and observation of their ability to communicate because, despite their best efforts, their patient satisfaction scores don't reflect their commitment to helping their patients. Should we be satisfied with our current level of performance, or should we as a profession always strive for a higher level? If I have mastered the clinical content of my field, can I then challenge myself to develop stronger communication skills with my patients and fellow clinicians?

Coaches are allied with a performer with the goal of helping the performer achieve the best performance possible. That said, there are numerous types and definitions of coaching.[2] Regardless of the specific model, several unifying themes emerge: (1) the critical importance of establishing an effective coach-coachee relationship, (2) attention to enhancing personal awareness and reflective capacity, (3) exploration of the coachee's goals, (4) a sober assessment of the coachee's current reality, and (5) enhancement of the coachee's self-sufficiency and will to grow. Professional coaching is a hot area these days and typically refers to a process whereby the coach uses powerful questions and other tools to enhance an individual's self-awareness and self-efficacy. With this sort of coaching, the coach does not provide content expertise to solve the coachee's problems but instead provides a structure and process by which clients come up with their own solutions. An emphasis is often placed on getting the client to focus on the future rather than on the past and, when contemplating the past, to focus on experiences of success that might reveal keys to succeeding in the future. In contrast, coaches in sports and the arts are expected to have high levels of content expertise and to be able to teach the content to players and performers. When professional tennis players hire a coach, they expect the coach to be deeply knowledgeable about both coaching and tennis. Communication skills coaching requires, in our view, a blend of these two types of coaching, whereby we leverage what the coachees already know, cultivate enhanced self-awareness, and facilitate the development of their own solutions, while also providing content expertise where needed.

An example of a common coaching model is G.R.O.W., which stands for identifying and developing coachee Goals; clearly assessing the coachee's current Reality; considering the coachee's Options for trying to achieve the identified goals; and Wrapping up by developing a strong action plan that takes into account practicality and obstacles.[3] Other similar models describe this as:

1. Imagining the ideal
2. Making a clear-eyed assessment of current reality
3. Developing a plan to close the gap between the current reality and the ideal
4. Articulating short-term plans that are specific, measurable, achievable, relevant to the longer-term goal of moving toward the ideal, and time-bound
5. Implementing the plans
6. Assessing their effectiveness

In a sense, then, coaching aims to bring a clear structure and accountability to the process of living one's life, a process that most of us conduct in an often disorganized, impulsive fashion if no one is there to provide a framework and hold us accountable.

Communication skills coaching adds some specific agenda items to this generic framework, and the items are grounded in our prioritization of building and attending to interpersonal relationships:

1. **Perception/observation skills.** We emphasize the importance of noticing and being able to name personality and behavioral cues so that the clinician can respond to the emotional state of the patient and colleagues. How, we need to ask ourselves, does this person before me seem to be feeling? What kind of day is he having? What can I learn about him simply by watching and listening?

2. **Rapport-building skills.** How do you make someone feel welcome? How do you make someone feel important? How do you establish trust? How do you start to make a connection?

3. **Empathic skills.** How do you let someone know that you care? How do you make her feel cared for? How can you begin to imagine what it would be like to be in the other person's situation? What are effective ways to respond to strong emotions? What does someone who is suffering experience as helpful?

4. **Listening skills.** How can you elicit the other person's story and perspective effectively? How can you listen so as to maximize the likelihood of accurately understanding what the other person is trying to say? How can you listen without hijacking or dominating the conversation?

5. **Explanatory skills.** How do you convey information in such a manner that it can be understood and remembered? How do you assess understanding?

6. **Negotiating and conflict-resolution skills.** What are your options for how to respond when conflict emerges? What are the pros and cons of these different options? How can you address conflict without escalating it? How can you use conflict as a path to a stronger relationship?

As noted earlier, our vision of communication and interpersonal skills coaching blends different coaching models in a way that some would call a combination of coaching and mentoring. We brought content expertise and thought that we were going to be most effective when we could facilitate a process by which the clinicians being coached arrived at their own solutions to the extent that they could. While in some coaching models the ideal is to have the coachees arrive at their own answers, coachees struggling with communication skills often benefit from examples of things to say and specific strategies to use. For example, one of the most powerful tools that our communication skills training participants tell us about is the "power of the pause," by which they mean waiting for the other person to speak or taking time to carefully formulate one's response. One coachee who was creating discord on teams by saying inflammatory things took to carrying a beverage around so that when tempted to respond in the heat of the moment, he could take a sip to prevent himself from speaking until he could consider his words more carefully.

> *Often it is more effective for us to learn what the other person has to say than for him or her to learn what we have to say.*

As we developed our approach to coaching, we were conscientious about linking it to the R.E.D.E. model and focusing on relational skills. In our communication courses, a key point of emphasis is attending to relationships. Entering an exam room to see a patient, the first priority for the clinician, barring a medical emergency, is the relationship. In coaching, the first priority for the coach is the relationship with the coachee because the work takes place in the context of that relationship. And when coaching, the most valuable help we can provide is to help the coachee develop more effective relational skills. Just as we want clinicians in our course to think about how to establish, develop, and engage in relationships with patients, so in coaching we want coachees to think about how to establish, develop, and engage in relationships in a variety of work settings.

Thus, the coaching process could be envisioned as moving through three stages: (1) establishing a connection with the person and negotiating an agenda; (2) developing the relationship by skillfully listening and asking powerful questions with the goal of enhancing both the coach's and the coachee's understanding of the coachee's goals and current reality; and (3) engaging the relationship by negotiating a plan of action and expectations of accountability. In the coaching setting, R.E.D.E. looks like the progression shown in Table 7.1.

R.E.D.E. in Coaching for Communication

We typically begin by meeting the coachee to start building a relationship. Often, this is done over coffee, breakfast, or lunch. Before tackling the issues at hand, we aim to learn who coachees are and how they ended up where they are. We also aim to help them understand what coaching is and what we have to offer. In the development phase, we explore their

TABLE 7.1 **R.E.D.E. to Coach**

Phase	Skill	With Patients	With Coachee
Phase I: Establishment	• Convey value and respect with welcome • Collaboratively set agenda • Convey empathy with S.A.V.E.	• Hi, I'm Dr. Gilligan. I'm glad to see you. Thanks for coming to see me. How are you today? • I'd like to get a list of your concerns that you want to address today. • You sound frustrated	• Hi, I'm Dr. Gilligan. I'm glad we were able to meet today, and I look forward to getting to know you. • I'd like to get a list of the different concerns that you are hoping to address with me. • It's hard to practice the way you want to sometimes.
Phase II: Development	• Elicit narrative • V.I.E.W. questions	• Tell me about your headaches from when they first started. • How are your headaches affecting your life? • What ideas do you have about what's wrong? Have you read about headaches on the Internet? • What are you hoping that I'll be able to do for you? • What are you most worried about?	• Help me understand how you ended up engaging in coaching? • How are the problems you discussed affecting your life? • What ideas do you have about what the problems are? • What are you hoping to get out of our work together? • What are you most worried about?
Phase III: Engagement	• Share diagnosis and information • Collaboratively develop a plan	• It looks like you are suffering from cluster headaches. Has anyone else ever suggested that to you? • What do you know about treatments for headaches?	• It sounds like you would like your patients to experience you as more caring than they do now. • What would that look like? What can you do to help them know that you care about them?

goals. What do they aspire to? What does success look like to them? When have they succeeded in the past? What strengths or assets did they use? What is their current reality? What do they like and dislike about it? What would they like to continue, and what would they like to change? Where are they succeeding, and where are they getting stuck? The engagement stage involves developing a plan for moving from the current reality toward the imagined ideal. What would it take to move in such a direction? What skills or assets could they deploy that would help them? What barriers do they foresee? What do they have to gain if they succeed? If their goal is for patients to feel fortunate to have them involved in their medical care and the reality is that their patient satisfaction scores are low, can they imagine what it would look or feel like to be a clinician who was beloved by his or her patients? How would such a clinician behave? How is that different from their current behavior? Although it may sound absurdly simple, applying the discipline to think about such matters systematically and without emotion or defensiveness can be powerful and transformative. Bolstering this process are the following key elements: the relationship, reflective capacity, external perspective, content expertise, and accountability.

The relationship

We strongly subscribe to the belief that effective coaching depends upon a trusting relationship with the person being coached. Entering into the coaching relationships with a sincere interest in and curiosity about who the people are, why they went into healthcare for a career, what they like and dislike about their work life, what they value, how they define success, what they are hoping for, and how they view their current struggles is important. On such a journey, it's important to trust your travel companion. The coach's goal is to help the coachee. Judging, criticizing, rehabilitating, reforming, and remediating are not the coach's responsibility or task assignment. If remediation is needed, and it often is, coaching can help individuals remediate their performance, but it is the individual's responsibility, not the coach's. The coach is there to support and to provide a structure and process, not to fix. The coach must also want the individual to succeed, and the coachee should feel this.

> *Coaching is, in a sense, an invitation to imagine a better future and then work toward it.*

Reflective capacity

Developing reflective capacity enables people to assess their own performance more accurately and to understand better both their impact on others and others' impact on them. We hope that clinicians will become more aware of how their specific behaviors affect other people and why they react the way they do to the behavior of others. How does it feel to an obese middle-aged woman dressed in her underwear to have a slim, athletic male physician tell her that she is fat? How does it feel to a doctor fiercely committed to improving the health of his patients when patients come in day after day with ever-increasing body mass indices and never-ending reasons why they haven't improved their diet, stopped smoking, or started an exercise regimen? In these instances, there are both cognitive and emotional frameworks underlying the logic of the interaction, and becoming more aware of the emotional elements is critical.

One day I saw a clinician treating a first-grade child who had tears streaming down her face in the middle of what the clinician expected to be a relatively painless procedure. The clinician said to the child, "Don't cry. Smile. It's not so bad." In a span of seven words, there were three statements that negated the emotion the child was feeling. Beyond that, the words communicated to the child not to feel what she was feeling. Later, when we debriefed, I recounted the incident to the clinician, who was surprised that he had said what he did. He reflected on it. "I think that when a patient is reacting to a procedure as if it's much more painful than I think it should be, I get angry at the patient." He recognized that the anger was inappropriate, and it was empowering for him to be able to name it. Armed with this insight, we brainstormed ways to manage his anger and develop language that was more attuned to the needs of the patient.

There is another reason that developing reflective capacity deserves prioritization: it is more effective to empower people to develop their own insights, goals, and solutions than to provide them with other people's insights, goals, and solutions. Sound familiar? We know that patients are more engaged in decisions that they are a part of making. Everyone is. If coachees depend on the coach's ideas, then how will they function when the coach isn't there to help? Coaching aims to enhance self-sufficiency and problem solving. Enhanced self-awareness combined with an ability to assess one's performance accurately through reflective processes helps achieve this aim.

External perspective

When a tennis coach watches someone serve or hit a backhand, she can see things that the player cannot see. We all tend to have both good and bad habits of which we are partly or entirely unaware. By shadowing or videotaping clinicians in action, performing 360-degree evaluations, and doing role-play exercises in which the clinician plays the role of the patient or colleague and hears her own words spoken to her, we can help individuals gain an external perspective on their behaviors and thus become more self-aware. As described by Windover in Chapter 5, external observation of their behavior or skill can move people from a place of unconscious incompetence to a place of conscious incompetence: now you know what you don't know. It is also the moment in one's learning process when skill building or training is useful because people are aware of areas they need to work on.

> *Only with awareness can someone make real changes to his or her behavior.*

In our coaching, we largely depend on shadowing and/ or videotaping to gain insight into these issues, although often much can be learned simply by listening and observing carefully. One physician we coached had colleagues complain that he made them feel stupid. When the coach sat down to talk with him, get to know him, and plan a coaching agenda, it struck him that the picture the coachee had drawn of the people he worked with was that they were not very good at their jobs and not very bright. Part of the behavior that was getting him into trouble was apparent if we watched for it and assessed our own response to his narrative. This makes it easier to start a conversation about his current reality and what a different reality might look like.

In today's world, we don't just have the external perspective of a coach; we have the external perspectives of the patients we serve. Comments on patient satisfaction surveys and patient complaints and compliments about a given provider to the ombudsman's office provide a wealth of information, and themes can emerge. Transparently highlighting these to providers can provide contextual information about potential blind spots and lead to a discussion of how the provider interprets these. How does feedback from patients compare to feedback from colleagues and coworkers? Most clinicians believe there is something unique about their patient population, and in some ways, this is undeniably true for everyone. And yet, unless they are planning on making a major professional change so that they see a completely different patient population, their patients are a reality in their world. We want to focus on how to work more effectively within that reality. An isolated complaint does not necessarily have much meaning, but where there are clear patterns and recurring themes, it is important to seek the meaning of the feedback.

Foundational knowledge about key communication skills

Content expertise is important because many useful skills and tools have been developed that are widely applicable and relatively easily applied. Clinicians need to be competent in a variety of communication tasks: listening and eliciting the patient's complaints and history; responding when a patient displays strong emotions; delivering bad news; educating patients about diagnoses and treatments in a manner that they can understand and retain the information; motivating patients to adopt healthy behaviors. The process of mastering these skills is often aided by providing learners with specific examples of what they might say that can be adapted by the individual and coach to fit more authentically with his or her personality and communication style.

Although we don't expect our clinicians to be experts in communication and the evidence surrounding it, we do want to build an expectation that core communication skills are important to their practice. Not all clinicians can generate the right words at the right time on their own. The benefit of working with a coach in a safe, private venue is that clinicians can be supported in developing their own language and approach. Not only are the core concepts in communication important, but how they are presented may also hold value. Given that all of our physicians have been required to undergo fundamental communication skills training, we aim in coaching to reinforce and build upon the skills taught in the R.E.D.E.-based courses. This maximizes the potential for encoding and recall.

We have found that most observed communication behaviors that are less effective and relatively easy to improve fall into a relatively small number of areas: listening, explaining, and empathy.

Take the example of the patient who is asking for narcotics that won't help him or a terminal cancer patient who has exhausted all treatment options. We commonly see polarizing positions that play out as follows:

PATIENT: Doc, I know I'm dying, but isn't there something you can do? You've got to do something.

DOCTOR: We are doing everything we can. I don't want you to spend your last few weeks upset or worrying. (tells patient not to worry when he or she is worrying)

PATIENT: Well, we can't just give up.

DOCTOR: I know. I just don't have anything left to offer. (doesn't provide any hope and isn't true—palliative care is something valuable to offer)

Compare that to:

PATIENT: Doc, I know I'm dying, but isn't there something you can do? You've got to do something.

DOCTOR: You sound like you want to keep fighting. (reflective listening and emotion naming)

PATIENT: Yeah, I guess I do. Doesn't everybody?

DOCTOR: Some people do. I wish I could fix all of this for you. In fact, I wish it wasn't happening to you. *Pause.* (reflective statement, two "I wish" statements, and a pause)

PATIENT: It's just been so hard. You've been there all along. (crying)

When we shadow clinicians, we are surprised by how much they talk when they are with patients. From a physician standpoint, they may feel they are conveying information about the disease state that is relevant to the patient and explaining things thoroughly. In most cases, from the patient perspective, it's too much and is not focused on what they most want to know. Most patients do not need to pass a board exam or become a content expert on their disease. Rarely do we hear patients asked what their current understanding of their condition is or what it is that they want to know. Open-ended questions are rarely utilized. The result is that patients get to tell only an abbreviated version of their story before they are buried in a blizzard of medical information. These explanations are like watching the clinician pour a gallon of liquid into an eight-ounce cup—most of the effort is wasted. Looking at it this way, it's easy to understand how physicians believe they are explaining a lot—which they are—but it's not necessarily what the patient wants explained nor is it in terms the patient can understand.

Our answer to this is more listening, less explaining, and targeting the explanation to what the patient wants to know or most needs to know. We recognize that the desire to give patients a detailed understanding of the pathophysiology of their condition is well intentioned, yet research shows that adults retain only a very small fraction of information that is provided in a lecture. It doesn't work. And the clock ticks away.

Regarding empathy, expressions of distress are often ignored or met with attempts to fix the distress. Rounding with a colleague one day, we entered the room of an elderly woman with advanced stage gastric cancer. She looked up from her bed and said, "Help me. Help me."

"What's the matter?"

"I'm in pain. I can't move."

"We're giving you medicine for pain. If you need more, you just need to ask for it."

So often we have seen this failure to express empathy for patient suffering and also a reflex to reach for a fix before fully understanding what is going on. What did this woman mean when she said she couldn't move? Couldn't move what? Why? Because of the pain? Had she suffered a neurological event? The weight of the responsibility to heal and fix patients seems to cause many of us to skip past empathy and understanding and reach instinctively for a solution. These reflexes can be unlearned. In the coaching context, we try to develop enhanced self-awareness and reflective competence on the one hand, and specific skills and tools that are helpful in building stronger relationships on the other.

Accountability

Coaching takes time and resources, and these investments must be accounted for. If coaching is to be utilized, then it is essential for it to provide demonstrable benefits. If a supervisor refers someone for coaching, it is with the hope and expectation that the coaching will result in improved performance. If someone self-refers, it is with the expectation that coaching will help achieve an outcome. Therefore, clearly defining the individual's goals for coaching and how progress will be assessed is necessary.

Similarly, it is the responsibility of the coachee to commit to participating wholeheartedly in the coaching process and working on the issues that led to coaching and to demonstrate implementation of the plan that is developed through the coaching process. If a coachee commits to videotaping three patient encounters and reviewing and assessing the resulting videos, then part of the coach's role is to hold the individual accountable for completing this work. If the coachee is not completing the agreed-upon work, then it is important to assess why and to reassess whether he or she is committed to the coaching process. If the work is being done but performance is not improving, however that is assessed, then the effectiveness of and/or appropriateness of the coaching should be reevaluated. Some people are less amenable to coaching, some coaches are not very effective, sometimes the pairing of the coach and the person being coached is problematic, and sometimes coaching is not an effective strategy for the specific issue being addressed.

The Coaching Process

Coaching is a process—a process that relies on the foundation of building a relationship of trust and mutual respect.

Referrals. Individuals are referred for communication skills coaching by either themselves or their supervisors. If they are referred by supervisors, we try to review whatever information can be shared about the reason for the referral, which may consist of patient satisfaction scores and comments or complaints, as well as information from supervisors or colleagues. Although this may risk biasing the coach, we have found such data to be essential to understanding why coaching has been requested. The coach then has a responsibility to remain unbiased and to remember that such data represents only part of the story.

Getting started. The initial meeting focuses on learning the individual's goals for coaching or understanding of why coaching was offered or recommended. The coach provides a description of the coaching process and ground rules. Many people are unfamiliar with coaching, so a basic review is appropriate. Ground rules for coaching emphasize confidentiality and a clear delineation of what, if any, information will be shared with others. If, for example, a supervisor refers someone for coaching, then it must be clear to all parties what if any information about the coaching will be shared with the supervisor and, if so, by whom. Such communication is typically limited to confirming that the individual is participating actively and making a good-faith effort in the coaching process. Ground rules also include how often coaching sessions will take place and what the two parties will expect from each other. Ground rules support the coaching relationship by helping to construct a safe environment characterized by shared expectations.

The second part of the initial meeting is getting to know the coachee. Curiosity is key. Good guiding questions for getting to know coachees include, What is it like to be them? What would it be like to go through a day as them? What makes them look forward to getting out of bed in the morning? What would they most like to change about their life? What are they most proud of? What experiences were key in their decision to enter into medicine? What is their family background, and how does it affect the way they behave in their current role?

Eliciting self-assessment. Defensiveness, self-doubt, insecurity, discomfort with vulnerability, and an exaggerated sense of humility or narcissism can all interfere with our ability to take our own measure. This is especially important when working with staff physicians because the culture of medicine inhibits our ability to acknowledge weakness and imperfection. Creating a safe environment in which to candidly reflect on the areas where one is more and less effective is critical. It is hard to improve if we don't have a reliable sense of what we need to work on. And it's hard to continue our successes if we have trouble identifying what it is that we have done effectively. So it is fruitful to ask people to reflect on the following: What do they view as their strengths and assets? When have they been successful in the past? What did they do to make those successes possible? What would they like to be more effective at? What is their understanding of why they are undergoing coaching? Do they feel that they have been unfairly criticized or singled out? If a problem has been identified, what is their understanding of the problem? Do they feel that they have contributed to it in any way?

Goal setting and making a plan. We have already raised the question of how coachees define success broadly. At this point, we are concerned with the goals for coaching. In the context of the issues that led to coaching, what are they hoping for? What would a successful outcome look like? We have already assessed their current reality, and now we want to consider what their ideal would look like. What is the gap between their reality and their ideal? What would it take to narrow that gap? How will we know whether the gap is closing? How will we measure progress?

It is critical here to separate long-term goals (such as improved patient satisfaction scores) and short-term goals that can be implemented and measured more immediately (such as consistently sitting down at the bedside and beginning by asking patients about their understanding of their condition). Once we have goals, we need a very specific plan that includes accountability. What exactly are they going to do? When are they going to do it? What measures are they going to report back? What will they do if the plan does not work? Perhaps the first goal is to use at least three empathic statements in every patient encounter or to practice letting patients talk for a full minute without interrupting.

The last time many clinicians got feedback on their communication probably was in medical school. It really isn't fair that we are pushed out into a world as staff—a world with higher expectations, more complexity, and great responsibility—and expected to have all the skills we need. Our perspectives change over the course of our career as a clinician. What we may need or want from a coach will be different at different stages. Most of us providing care take great pride in it, and it hurts us in many ways when our patients don't know how much we care. A coach can bridge the gap.

Power Points

1. Use coaching when clinicians want or need more individualized attention than can be provided in a small group class.

2. Coaching builds on a foundation of a strong, trusting, appreciative, and candid relationship.

3. Increasing personal awareness in clinicians through coaching allows them to come up with their own solutions.

4. Don't get stuck in definitions. Blend elements of professional coaching and mentoring for maximum impact.

Facilitating Staff Physicians Is Not the Same as Teaching Residents or Students . . . Or Is It?

I'll be lucky if I graduate with a kernel of empathy left.

—NEUROSURGERY CHIEF RESIDENT

We hope you've started to envision how the facilitation techniques we've presented can enhance the facilitation that you are already doing, or will hopefully be doing soon. Although there has been a lot of research on the training of medical students and residents, it is less certain whether these strategies and approaches translate into the world of practicing clinicians, attending physicians in particular. Often, we assume they do. In our experience, we developed different approaches for them that helped us tailor our training to their needs. In this chapter, we will discuss communication training for residents and fellows and highlight areas of consideration when facilitating for this group.

The Case for Similarity

Medical students and residents become staff physicians, so the internal motivations and training framework are similar. Resident and fellow (trainee) training in communication appears to be the same as teaching attending physicians in the following ways:

- The foundational skills for relationship building are the same.
- The themes for communication challenges are the same.
- Both often think they do a pretty good job of communicating with patients already.
- Both are scientists who critically evaluate evidence.
- Their time is valuable.
- They bring their own values and experiences to bear.
- Both feel vulnerable when their communication skills are criticized.
- Neither group becomes better communicators by listening to lectures on how to communicate.
- Both frequently evolve in a deficit-based culture.

The Case for Differences

We already know that empathy declines in medical school and residency as pressures escalate during training. Not only does it decline, it doesn't recover until late in one's medical career. Efforts to better understand the environment of our medical students and residents offer several reflections about what is different for these populations:

- Trainees are much more likely to have had communication skills training in medical school than faculty.
- Trainees have had less clinical time and experience with patients.
- Trainees have basic needs that aren't necessarily met (sleep, food, etc.).
- Trainees are at a different stage of life, both personally and professionally.
- Attendings have the final say in the plan of care; trainees don't.
- Trainees are expected to teach each other.
- Because they are lower on the medical hierarchy (with less power), trainees may be made to feel as though their opinions will not be taken into consideration.
- An attending facilitator may be perceived as an adversary rather than a peer.
- Trainees are still in learning mode and therefore seem excited to be challenged intellectually.

Resident and Fellow Communication Training: Current State

While recently facilitating a group of nine residents, we noted that all of the residents had had some form of communication training; at least half had participated in role-play, and four said they had been videotaped during patient encounters and were given feedback. When the same question is posed to attendings, few mention prior training.

Many medical students today are being educated in institutions that give time and importance to communication skills and to the relationships that are essential to a productive medical career. Medical students today are likely not only to have been trained with skills practice regularly incorporated into their learning, but also to have had more of this formal training than any physician that has been in practice for 25 years.[1] In a 2011 survey of medical schools in the United States, 97 percent of schools surveyed reported that they use simulation to give feedback on interpersonal communication skills, and 78 percent use simulation as an assessment tool. In residency, these numbers are 85 and 47 percent respectively.[2]

Understanding the Most Basic Needs

Maslow postulated that before a person is able to reach a level of higher learning, his or her basic physiologic needs such as food, water, and rest must be met.[3] Meeting these needs provides the platform essential to creating safety, belonging, confidence, and reflection. This may seem like common sense; however, residents and fellows come to the communication class having put their needs last on the list, in lieu of the needs of their patients and their clinical services. This was borne out in our observations of resident classes: much of the meet-and-greet time was spent eating. Yes, eating. It would be a simple conclusion to say they just eat more, but a more thoughtful theory would be that trainees are taught to "eat when you can" or that the eating is a stress response to their environments and pressures. Subsequently, we increased the amount of food served for a resident class as compared to the attending class—and it almost always is eaten. Understanding, anticipating, and addressing the stressors sets everyone up for success.

> *People cannot learn until their basic needs are met.*

Attending to the basic physiologic needs of participants is a cornerstone of our program and relationship-centered approach. Recognizing that residents and students have different needs than attendings may make all the difference in their engagement. Like attending physicians, trainees may have had to round on patients in the morning prior to the communication class, may have been on call the night before, or may have to return to the hospital to check on patients immediately after the class. This deserves attention and adaptation. Remembering that the person with the heavy eyelids at 2 p.m. is the person who has had little sleep, and not someone who considers you a boring facilitator, is the facilitation skill of simply meeting people where they are without judgment. Many residents, especially those in surgical specialties, have to get to the hospital at 4 a.m. to start seeing patients. Senior residents often go back to the hospital to check on the medical students, interns, and residents on their team to see if there is anything left undone. Although it seems more common among trainee groups, any clinician in any class may have been on call the night before, had early and late rounding, or something else. We often call these issues out during our warm-up questions so we can understand participants' readiness to learn and adapt our approach and expectations for them.

I'm Just Trying to Remember My Address

According to data from the American Association of Medical Colleges, the average U.S. resident graduates medical school and begins internship at the age of 28.[4] In addition, the U.S. Census Bureau shows that the average age of marriage for a male is 28.5 and for a female is 26.5.[5] The average college-educated woman is 28.2 years old when she has her first child, and the college-educated male is 30.8. The average age of first-time home buyers is 31. Thirty-four percent of medical students enter medical school in debt, and the median amount of those debts is $20,000. Eighty-four percent of medical students leave medical school in debt, with the median amount being $176,000.[6] These statistics highlight the stage-of-life issues confronting residents.

Let's take a minute to envision this more fully. Jennifer is a 27-year-old woman who just graduated from medical school and is about to start residency. She completed medical school in the same city where she did her undergraduate training, so she had friends in the area during her medical school career. She was invited to various bridal showers and weddings of these friends. In the later years of medical school, baby showers started to trickle onto her social calendar. Because of the demands of medical school, she was not able to make all of these events. Some of her friends understood. Others did not. She had a boyfriend for some of this time, but he had to take a job in a different city and they both felt that the long-distance relationship wouldn't work for them: he would be too busy establishing his career, and she would be too busy studying and doing hospital rotations.

Jennifer was ready to go to residency training. She found a program that she really admired and that would further her professional development. The only drawback was that it was in a new city where she didn't know anyone. She soon discovered that she was living in a nice area, but most of the other residents from the hospital lived in the other direction from her apartment. She worked weekends for the first two months, so she wasn't able to travel away from the city. Her good friends from home couldn't travel because they were either taking care of their kids, working weekends in their own residency positions, or couldn't justify spending the money. Although the other residents in the program were nice, Jennifer didn't know them well, and most of them had a significant other, fiancé, or spouse.

As highlighted by Jennifer's story, residents are dealing with tremendous personal adjustment and life changes while trying to master the content of medicine. Residency is a time when you are taking all of the facts that you learned in medical school and trying to make them fit into the context of the living patient in your care. With all of this happening at once, the skills of communication and building a relationship with the patient can be given a lower priority. With the collision of personal and professional events, residents are in a place where they need support and empathy of their own. After facilitating a resident course, one of our facilitators commented that the residents seemed to need more empathy throughout the day than any class that he had ever facilitated for attendings. Residents, like other clinicians, are often patients. Powerful stories have emerged in our sessions about cancer survival, loss, holding dying children, seeing death for the first time and no one discussing it, miscarriages, watching their parents die. Our trainees often enter medicine because they carry their own scars.

The Reality of Relationships on Rounds

When you think about the type of work that most residents are being asked to do and the way they are being asked to do it, you quickly realize that relationship building is not on their task list. Residents are asked to have quick communication on morning rounds, often seeing up to 10 patients an hour. They rarely, if ever, are congratulated for relationship building, especially if it means they didn't get their other work done.

Medical knowledge, diagnostic acumen, and safety are top priorities in training, and not without reason. On rounds, the clinical focus is often on vital signs, lab tests, imaging results—all of which will enhance their medical knowledge, diagnostic acumen, and recognition of patient safety. Yet medical students and trainees are expected to learn the art of medicine by observation. If they are not asked which communication skill will help lessen the patient's anxiety or which empathic statement they can use after telling the patient she has cancer, these skills won't be reinforced.

There is a lot of discussion surrounding the hidden curriculum of medical training, which encompasses everything, often unflattering things, trainees learn that we didn't intend to teach.[7] In terms of communication skills, residents frequently shadow attendings who have not participated in formal communication skills training and who may not prioritize or value empathic, relationship-centered communication. Of course there are those who do value these skills. The students and residents who *did* receive this training were taught the skills and yet do not see these skills being used, valued, or recognized in everyday practice. The underlying message in the hidden curriculum, therefore, is that these communication skills are not important to be a successful physician. This is one of the reasons that residents were not included in the initial focus of our communication training. We didn't want them to learn skills that subsequently were messaged to be unimportant. By the time the residents took the R.E.D.E. to Communicate: FHC course, at least one-third of their attendings had been trained in these skills.

In addition to dealing with the hidden curriculum, trainees are often criticized or berated for making any type of mistake during their medical training. Criticism can come after a resident missed an important lab value just as easily as it can come from that same resident arguing with a patient about a plan of care. Some attendings will actively undermine the relationship between the resident and the patient on rounds by saying to the patient, "You don't have to listen to Dr. Youngin since I'm the one who has the final say. He's just learning." Another physician told us that when he rounded at a large academic hospital system as a resident, the attending would turn to him and say, "Now let's hear from someone whose opinion doesn't really matter." Trainees may not have anyone offering encouragement when they catch important lab values or when they decide to use reflective listening and empathy to discuss a difference of opinion on a plan of care. Instead, we often focus on what went wrong.

Consider this scenario: A patient comes into the emergency room with severe abdominal pain, suspected to be appendicitis. Josh, a second-year resident working in the emergency department, orders a CT scan of the patient's abdomen to confirm appendicitis and to see if the patient needs surgery. The patient refuses to get into the CT scanner. Josh spends an extra 20 minutes getting to know the patient's situation, listening to his biggest fears, and eliciting the main barriers to a plan of care. In doing so, Josh discovers that the patient's grandfather was diagnosed with metastatic colon cancer after a CT scan, and the patient is terrified that the doctors think he has cancer, too. After Josh effectively uses communication skills to build a relationship, the patient agrees to a CT scan, appendicitis is confirmed, and the patient has surgery to prevent worsening complications from the appendicitis. In a busy emergency department or in your hospital, will Josh be celebrated for his efforts or told that ER wait times are increasing and to move it along?

The communication challenges that both residents and attendings say they are facing are similar: dealing with an angry patient, managing unrealistic expectations, giving bad news, and so on. However, the details that lead to these encounters may be quite different. Again, because they are lower on the traditional medical hierarchy, residents are often tasked with communicating with families after something has gone wrong or wasn't handled in the best way, situations that residents didn't create and can't control but that nonetheless expose them to the emotional torrent from patients and family members. Or it's the middle of the night, and they are covering another team's service and are called by the nurse to speak with an angry patient they have never met.

The details surrounding unrealistic expectations also may highlight a resident's plight. A patient may no longer have active issues keeping her in the hospital, yet the patient resists discharge. The attending is usually the one who makes the decision that the patient has to leave but often delegates to the resident the task of communicating to the patient that she is being discharged. When the resident tells the patient that she has to leave the hospital, the patient may get upset, cry, yell, or give a really good reason why she needs to stay. The resident, however, has been given orders that the patient has to leave the hospital and was not told that compromise is an option. That resident has to deal with either an unhappy patient or an unhappy attending. Neither situation feels like a job well done.

Teaching While Being Taught

Residents and fellows have teaching responsibilities as they go through training. As you facilitate this group, allow this fact to work to your advantage. Previous chapters have discussed our small group facilitation technique that ensures that we are spending time highlighting effective behaviors. With the resident group, one of the ways to combine positive reinforcement and their teaching responsibilities is to say, "I hope that when you have medical students with you, you are making sure to point out that it was your use of silence that allowed the patient to open up and tell his story" or "Has anyone told you before that your smile when greeting the patient, and summarizing his last few days in the hospital, really help the patient trust you in the first few seconds of an encounter? Think about how you might highlight this to other team members that are learning from you."

Given the amount of previous training that residents and fellows have had, we are very intentional in using the word *facilitator*, not *teacher*, when referring to those running the course. We do this partly to stay humble in our role, but mostly to recognize that every participant in our course has experiences from which we can learn, including the facilitator. There is an inherent power dynamic present in a class of trainees, and for some facilitators, humility and recognition of helpful experience can be difficult skills to model. Multiple types of power exist, and attendings may possess power because of their title or leadership role, as well as their content knowledge. This power may play itself out in a variety of ways with trainees, and awareness of it is critical to success.

In the first few months training residents, one of the communication classes didn't go so well and was frustrating for two very skilled facilitators. When I asked one of the facilitators about the course, her comments can be paraphrased as "Who do those residents think they are, being disrespectful to my cofacilitator and myself? We are attending physicians, and they should have given us at least that much respect and listened to what we have to say." They went on to talk about how the residents don't have the same amount of clinical experience or even life experience.

It was extremely helpful to hear these comments because they highlighted the unconscious bias that facilitators can bring to trainee groups without knowing it. Often, facilitators will see an attending-level physician who challenges the data that we present as an *expected yet reasonable* "naysayer" or "forced marcher" who needs time, practice, and the opinion of a colleague to open himself up to the skills we are offering. Yet this same participant may be perceived as "insubordinate" in the resident group and someone who needs to be taught a lesson in respect.

The ability of facilitators to maintain self-awareness about how they are feeling about the reaction of participants, what that is triggering in them, and their ability to register these feelings and put them aside so that they can meet the residents where they are is paramount. Regardless of our titles or years of experience, we all want to be respected and valued. In fact, it is a beautiful parallel between what patients want from us. Just because they don't know all the medicine and are in a gown doesn't mean they are deserving of any less respect. It is important to find a way to communicate respect for the resident or trainee experience early when facilitating with this group. We often ask residents to help make sure the class is relevant for future participants, requesting that they point out similarities and differences in our courses to their prior communication skills training.

Key Strategic Approaches to Trainees

We identified a subgroup of facilitators who enjoy working with the residents preferentially. This group may be earlier in their training or may work closely with residents in other settings. We sent a checklist to the facilitators before their first three resident courses to remind them of some of the facilitation skills that will help them connect with the resident group. These key strategic approaches will be discussed in the following section. Comments from our facilitators after working with the resident group reveal that with the right attitude and approach by the facilitator, the resident classes are invigorating, energizing, and a whole lot of fun. One facilitator told me, "A bit of off-color humor probably went a long way, but banter and humility were probably worth more."

The communication curriculum for most medical schools is introduced in the first year and is built upon over time. If Jennifer, from the previous story, was asked how to get to the grocery store in her new town or to remember the mnemonic on how to elicit a patient narrative, it is easy to imagine that directions to the grocery store will take a higher priority. It is for this reason that we currently teach R.E.D.E. to Communicate to new residents starting in September of their first year rather than during their orientation. The time from July to September allows residents to adjust to their new life and their new role. It also gives them more clinical time with patients. In this way, they are able to come to class having experienced the pressure of these conversations as a new doctor.

Trainees are used to being in the role of learner, and they are hungry to master their specialty. As such, they are often more engaged and more willing to practice techniques differently. Facilitators need to make sure that they come prepared for anything. In the class of nine resident participants who all had very robust prior training in communication skills, we found the learning edge (the place between boredom and feeling overwhelmed) of each participant and made sure we were challenging that edge. One of the small group scenarios that day was breaking bad news to a patient. Another involved talking to a patient when a disruptive family member was present. These are scenarios that would be too advanced for first-time learners in another setting.

In some other classes, the resident participant who had been videotaped in medical school may be sitting next to someone who has only received lectures on communication skills. As facilitators, one of our roles is to create safety while making the session meaningful. We wouldn't want the resident who received only lectures to be worried that his or her small group skills practice session will involve breaking bad news to a patient and the patient's hostile spouse just because the previous resident identified that as his or her learning edge. One of the ways to engage a group with different skill levels is to ask the very skilled participants to help you pay attention to those communication skills they have learned previously; invite them to help you cofacilitate in a sense.

There is benefit in having these classes be a mix of years of experience and specialty, just as with the attending-level classes. Early in the expansion of these skills to the resident group, we had a class that consisted of 12 residents all from the same specialty. Instead of being an experience in which the communication skills could be adapted to that single specialty, it became a matter of "You don't know what it's like in *our* world," and the residents highlighted all the reasons why the skills wouldn't work for them. The facilitators were not from the same specialty and were seen as lacking in credibility. When friends are sitting next to each other, instead of new acquaintances, there is less filtering of unprofessional comments. This seemed to be the situation that we were facing in training a small group of residents who all knew each other. When the classes contain a mix of specialties, you are less likely to have an entire group feel suspicious and mistrustful and intrepid enough to be vocal about it.

To make sure that mixing resident specialties and postgraduate year (PGY) levels is acceptable to trainees, we asked them their preference after taking the course. On the questionnaire, residents were given the option of having the course with the same specialty and same PGY level; the same specialty and a mix of PGY levels; a mix of specialties and same PGY level; a mix of specialties and mix of PGY levels; and no preference. Our results found that 53 percent of residents preferred taking the course with a mix of specialties and PGY levels, while 32 percent had no preference.

Nostalgic

At the end of every class, we ask participants for a word or a phrase to describe how they are feeling as a result of the day. Our favorite word came from a surgical resident. His word was "nostalgic." In describing this more fully, the resident said that a day spent focused on building relationships with our patients through communication made him remember all of the great reasons that he went into the medical field in the first place.

Another neurology resident shared that spending time on hospital service with one of our facilitators had gotten him thinking. "I've started identifying patients by their room number. I used to have a dream. I was going to provide medical care, and my wife, a music therapist, was going to join me in providing meaningful, healing care for those less fortunate. I haven't thought about that dream in a long time."

Getting our physicians to dream again just may be our greatest outcome.

Power Points

1. Appreciate that residents and attending physicians are at different life stages, which is relevant to how and what they learn.

2. Seize the moment! One significant advantage for residents, fellows, and medical students is that they are already in learning mode.

3. Celebrating micromoments of effective relationship building and communication on rounds represents an enormous opportunity.

4. Customize. When developing programs for trainees, consider timing, selection of interested facilitators, and responsiveness to their real-world challenges.

5. Engage with humor, humility, and self-awareness, and be mindful of any power differentials in the group.

Chapter 9

Who Facilitates Whom?

Advanced Care Provider Training

*Thank goodness you didn't have a
nonphysician teach this course.*

This comment came from a participant in one of our
sessions for doctors within the first year of the rollout.
It's not a comment that any program or organization
wants to hear, yet it wasn't uncommon. It's interesting that
the term *nonphysician* was used, as few of us define ourselves
by what they are not. How many Asian male physicians call
themselves nonwhite, nonfemale non-nurses? Beyond the issue
of language, it's easy to come to the conclusion that physicians
think that no other professionals have the same knowledge
base and experience that they do. Some physicians do feel this
way, and programs that focus on relationship-centered communication rather than just physician-patient communication
have a role in helping this thinking evolve. However, if we

stay in a place of empathic curiosity, there are other options to explore. In an era when there is increasing emphasis on teams and interprofessional communication, the attitude that doctors are "different" feels outdated. Comments like the one above opened up a critical dialogue about how training or profession can affect perception of the course's benefits.

We've described much of our work with staff physicians because we targeted that group early on. As the program evolved, however, we made a concerted effort to integrate our training and our facilitators with advanced care providers (ACPs) and physicians. This chapter will explore our experience training ACPs in separate courses from physicians and our decision to move to more integrated courses.

The Who and Why

Our communication skills courses were initially taught separately to physicians, on the one hand, and physician assistants (PAs), nurse practitioners (NPs), and additional ACPs on the other. The physician group included MD/DOs and was taught by their peers, MD/DO facilitators. Likewise, the ACP group was also taught by their peers. The decision to group the courses in this way was an intentional one. The rationale for differentiating physician training from ACP training was based on several considerations: physicians and ACPs would feel safer practicing communication skills in front of their peers. Physicians might feel embarrassed looking less than competent in front of ACPs, and ACPs might fear disrespectful behavior from physicians. Safety is paramount, and we value it even more than the benefits of interprofessional training. Think for a minute about a scenario in which physicians object to having a nurse practitioner facilitating their course. They become vocal about the nurse practitioner not understanding their unique, daily job challenges and disengage actively from the training. The course easily can become about managing *their* issue, when it is really intended to strengthen the communication skills of the entire group. We wanted to make participants feel safe and supported so that they could engage in the training—and part of that safety was honoring the sacredness of the conversations physicians have with patients and the conversations advanced care providers have. We also were aware that it might be equally problematic to have a physician lead communications skills training for a group of NPs. We prioritized the participants above all else, and for our culture at that time, it was the right strategy. In addition, the first physicians to take the course during the roll-out phase were those whom we wanted to master and model the skills for colleagues and trainees. We hypothesized that both groups would find greater validity if the content came from peers. We worried about pushback in the form of "You don't understand what it's like to do my job." A peer-to-peer format seemed most likely to reduce resistance, although we recognized that it deprived us of the opportunity to work on interprofessional communication issues in a way that an integrated approach would. So, using R.E.D.E to Communicate: FHC as the foundational prerequisite course, we subsequently built advanced courses that integrated physicians and ACPs.

For ACP FHC classes, we originally sought to identify those who had substantial patient contact. In the initial discussions, this included nurse practitioners, as well as physician assistants. However, as the course continued, we soon found that we had an audience of PhDs, PAs, advanced practice nurses, certified nurse specialists, certified registered nurse anesthetists (CRNAs), perfusionists, physical and occupational therapists, speech therapists, dentists, podiatrists, optometrists, and dieticians, to name a few. We accommodated almost anyone with the understanding that our target audience performed direct patient care, was working with patients routinely, and was comfortable participating in the skills practice exercises. We initially included those individuals who had a National Provider Identifier (NPI) number on our target list of folks who should participate. Everyone with an NPI is a billing provider and has direct patient care contact. The list is easy to compile and keep track of within a large healthcare system.

The How of ACP FHC Training

In one course, a nurse practitioner, who worked in a 24-hour nursing call center, reported never actually interfacing with people in person. Instead, she exclusively talked with people on the phone. She was the only one in the class who did not see patients in a clinic setting and reported that she was uncomfortable in the skills practice portion. She expressed resistance and negativity about the class at first, which is understandable if you don't think it applies to you! Our challenge was to find out what specifically made her uncomfortable and brainstorm with her how the skills applied. In the demonstration, we put two chairs together, back to back. The simulated patient and ACP sat in these chairs, which replicated the real-world experience of the nurse. She immediately felt more at ease, and we had a productive exploration of how and where the skills applied in her world. Creativity and flexibility were keys to our success in the ACP courses.

As illustrated, a significant challenge facilitating courses for ACPs is the variety of settings and types of interactions that they may have with patients. This led to creative and innovative ideas for skills practice sessions constructed to closely resemble the participant's environment and challenges. Understanding this need and being flexible and able to adapt the case on the spot requires a talented facilitator; this resulted in lasting and profound rewards. Adapting the case and helping the participant step into a more realistic role is a way to relieve anxiety and facilitate effective skills practice. If the participants are ACPs who mainly work in pre- and post-op areas, and they are asked to practice communication skills in the context of seeing a patient in clinic, their discomfort rises and is prohibitive to the learning process. They become distracted, worrying about identifying the best treatment. By adapting to what providers know and the setting in which they practice, the facilitator enables them to fully engage in the process and focus on communication skills.

Standard cases can be adapted in a variety of ways to meet the specific needs of the clinical care providers and other caregivers. The cases can be adapted with regard to who attends the appointment with the patient, the circumstances surrounding the patient encounter (emotions, specialty, problem), and where the encounter takes place (phone, front desk, office, inpatient setting). For example, some of the other case adaptations involved parents bringing in their children, adult children bringing in their parents or senior parents, and family members bringing in non-English-speaking family members or friends. These cases focus not only on the patient but on treating the entire family system. This type of adaptation often requires participants to take on these roles and mirrors the actual complexity of issues that all caregivers face.

Another example of an adaptation involved the dietitians and nutritionists, particularly those who work in our Employee Health Plan (EHP) Program. They reported challenges related to treating employees and family members of employees who used their services as part of the EHP. In our organization, efforts have been made to reduce the cost of the EHP through employee engagement in preventative health programs and activities. Our dietitians routinely indicated that many of those visits were difficult because patients felt they were being forced into participating. By building a case with these basic features and then applying the R.E.D.E. skills, the dietitians were able to see the value of the skills to their primary communication challenge. An additional, unforeseen benefit to this group was the opportunity to air these challenges and discuss management options. We could see the stress on their faces and feel the anger as they shared the frustrations they had been dealing with silently. This spurred empathy and encouragement from the group. The group developed ideas and shared insights on how best to apply the R.E.D.E. skills, and the dietitians received validation.

Despite the diversity and differences in duties among different ACPs, each provider deals daily with core communication challenges such as breaking bad news, strong emotions, and unrealistic expectations. The medical issues of the case or the setting are not as relevant in this training as the emotional ones. The skills practice emphasizes a focus on the emotion at the core of the communication challenge, which is shared by all providers, no matter what degree is after one's name.

Although ACPs ultimately engaged in the course and rated it very favorably, they were "healthy skeptics," as we call them. When they arrived to take the course, they expressed it would be a "waste of time" or asserted that they were already well trained. We endorsed lifelong learning and also sought out "cofacilitators" in the audience to balance these expressions, rather than argue with them directly. To engage them, we also had to demonstrate benefit and applicability to their particular role by facilitating skills practice based on their work settings. The experiential piece was often the most eye-opening to participants, and so we moved them into these phases quickly. When they play the role of the provider and/or the patient, they feel the impact of the words chosen; there really is no substitute for that experience. As much as they may not have wanted to participate in the skills practice portion, on the postsurvey, we consistently heard positive comments about its impact:

"The role-play—even though I hate doing it myself, that's when I learned the most."

"Role-playing, uncomfortable but valuable."

"Role-playing and also giving input on others' role-playing."

"The interactive group sessions. Getting the chance to practice skills."

With longer follow-up, participants reported that interactions with patients are more personally rewarding after taking the course, in part due to a more efficient use of their time because of more effective communication skills. Lack of time, regardless of the individual's position, is routinely one of the most common issues providers discuss during the course. Facilitators benefit from showing how skills do not take more time but actually make the visit more efficient and effective.

Participant feedback also has focused on the safety of the space, the relevance to their own practice, and the common universal themes in communication challenges. The following are typical comments:

"All content was relevant to my clinical practice. This course provides the foundational elements for a cure for what ails medical care . . . establishment of a genuine effective relationship between patient and provider."

"Agenda building, empathetic expression, reflective listening."

"Reflective listening, the relationship model, and people's experiences."

"I thought my communication with patients was excellent prior to this, but I think it will improve greatly after this."

"Nonjudgmental atmosphere. Nonintimidating environment."

"I really feel like my communication skills will be much more effective with patients and fellow staff."

Two words from participants that recurred over and over, year after year, were "safe" and "supported." Whether participants vocalized this feedback directly to the facilitator or wrote it in the evaluations, the power of the environment created in the room was palpable throughout the day. At times, the clinicians shed tears, became emotional, and revealed to the group some of their greatest struggles, wishes, and regrets in their interactions with patients.

One participant entered the class expressing verbally and nonverbally, "I don't need this." He crossed his arms and stated several times, "I don't have time for this. My time is too important to be doing this." By the end of the class, however, he reflected on his strengths and weaknesses and allowed himself to be vulnerable enough to say, "I need help with giving patients bad news." Clinicians, even those who are initially resistant, often admit obtaining great value from the class because they were able to practice the skills and receive feedback from their peers who share similar challenges in their day-to-day work. It's apparent that this "safe" and "supported" environment is essential.

Over time, as our culture evolved and the course developed a strongly positive reputation, we became more confident that we could create a safe environment for more diverse and integrated groups of participants. If the primary goal was to improve healthcare communication—and we know much of healthcare is conducted in a multiprofessional environment—then pairing physician and ACP facilitators and integrating physician and ACP participants would be helpful and important.

What to Consider when Launching an Interprofessional Program

Education and background

Physicians and ACPs often report having had different types and levels of training and various experiences practicing their communication skills in their roles. For example, ACPs often have more extensive training and backgrounds in communication skills. PAs spend an average of six years in college and graduate school, the first four years completing undergraduate studies and the next two years toward their master's degree. NPs are similar in that they must first obtain their RN-BSN, which is also a four-year degree. Additionally, they must practice as an RN for one to two years before enrolling in a master's program, which is one to three years, depending on the specialty. The curriculum has a heavy emphasis on developing interpersonal and communication skills, which encompass verbal, nonverbal, written, and electronic exchanges of information. Throughout their education, ACPs must demonstrate skills that result in effective information exchanges with patients, their families, physicians, peers, and other professionals within the healthcare system. These skills are measured and evaluated objectively as core competencies during their course work and the practical clinical rotations of their training.

In contrast, physicians typically spend eight years in college and medical school before three or more years of postgraduate training as residents. They complete some coursework on communication and interpersonal skills, but this has, until recently, been extremely limited for most physicians. Many complete five to seven years of postgraduate training without ever formally revisiting these skills. According to one review, less than 5 percent of the physician curriculum time is spent on communication skills training.[1]

During the residential years, when the physicians specialize in a particular medical discipline, even less attention is given to the subject.

Once they have graduated and start working, ACPs continue to engage regularly in communication and relationship-focused seminars and training. This is in part due to their role as patient educators. In the traditional setting, physicians diagnose and develop a treatment plan. They may impart that information to the patient succinctly and move on to the next room. For a variety of reasons, schedules often are constructed such that physicians have less time in the room with patients than ACPs do, and in such instances, the physician may rely on a seasoned nurse or ACP to help patients understand the information and address their questions. Thus, ACPs have multiple opportunities to practice and hone their skills daily. Whether it's obtaining a history, explaining a diagnosis and treatment plan, or giving therapeutic instruction, the ACP may serve as the anchor for patients and their loved ones. An increasing number of ACPs are running their own clinics daily, seeing patients, diagnosing and delivering information and education, and developing patient relationships.

Tension

Despite increasing attention on interprofessional communication and education, data suggests tension in the physician and ACP relationship. This was discussed in a recent study published in the *New England Journal of Medicine* that highlighted that many nurse practitioners believed they should be in charge of the medical home.[2] When asked whether physicians performed a higher quality exam and consultation than NPs, there was a discrepancy among the responses, indicating that the vast majority of physicians believe this to be true, whereas 75 percent of nurse practitioners disagreed. If ACPs often feel they are doing the same job as physicians and not receiving the same benefits, then the stage is set for tension and resentment. Recent literature has brought this issue to the forefront. In one study, 30 percent of residents reported bullying behaviors by their nursing colleagues, most commonly in the form of being ignored by them when they approach.[3] Similarly, we hear stories of nurses suffering backlash from physicians because they called an ethics consult or the emergency response team when they became concerned for a patient. In one study, 31 percent of nurses reported feeling bullied in the workplace, and this was associated with their leaving the organization.[4] From a communication skills program standpoint, interprofessional tensions are important to recognize and to actively seek out, as it may be insulting or threatening to some ACPs to put a physician facilitator in front of them for a communication course just as the converse may also be true. Our belief is that the path forward is for different types of clinicians to cultivate a curiosity about and an understanding of the experience of others. Replacing judgment with curiosity is a key pathway toward forming authentic relationships, improving engagement and resiliency, and managing conflict in a productive manner.

Power

Power differentials matter, and they can threaten the clinician's perception of safety. Power differentials can also threaten patient safety if they prevent clinicians from speaking up or otherwise communicating critical information. In the book *What Keeps Leaders Up at Night*, Lipkin discusses how power can be perceived or real, and can manifest as different types, including coercive, expert, legitimate, reward, and referent power.[5] When different professionals work together, these power differentials, whether real or perceived, can significantly distract from learning. When power, hierarchy, and diversity factors are present, emotional issues and needs often rise to the surface and individuals can become emotionally hijacked. While this can represent an opportunity to work on these critical issues, it can also distract from other important agendas in a foundational communication skills course. Balancing these competing issues and recognizing the implications of any course format is the name of the game. Ultimately, thoughtfulness and sensitivity to emotional and psychological safety are required, no matter what format is chosen.

ACP advantages

There are pros and cons to teaching within or across professions. Several studies indicate that physicians and other medical professionals can be trained together to help patient care be seamless, to improve outcomes, and to acknowledge that a team, rather than one provider, is responsible for the patient. Interprofessional education is receiving increasing attention as an important type of training in healthcare, given that team approaches to care are increasingly the norm.[6]

As noted earlier, communication skills are more heavily emphasized in ACP training, education, and work flow, and ACPs often are allotted more time with patients. It is not surprising then that there are perceived differences in the care provided by an ACP and a physician. Overall, ACPs receive higher patient satisfaction scores compared to physicians (internal data). The differences are small, but they are consistent across multiple domains: provider gave clear information, 95.1 percent versus 93.0; provider spent enough time, 96.6 percent versus 92.9; provider knows my medical history, 91.1 versus 88.4; provider explained, 96.8

versus 94.1; provider listened, 97.2 versus 94.6; and provider respects me, 97.4 versus 95.8. These differences may be reflective of the team approach to healthcare infiltrating inpatient and outpatient environments, with ACPs increasingly being delegated to performing the bulk of follow-up communication and responding to patient phone calls or e-mails. If patients are able to communicate or make a request directly to the ACP, they may get a response more quickly and more reliably.

Several factors may contribute to these differences. As mentioned, scheduling may give physicians less time with patients, and much of the communication may be delegated to ACPs. In addition, ACPs may take a more holistic approach to the patient. Often, they know more about what is going on with patients besides their primary medical problem. If the ACP has spent more time with the patient and is more accessible by phone and e-mail, the patient may feel a stronger connection with the ACP. Second, ACPs receive substantial course work, clinicals, and training on the value of patient education and the importance of conveying detailed, understandable information and instruction to patients. Third, ACPs on average may be more prone than physicians to emphasize relationship building as central to their role. Many ACPs voice expecting this relationship and seeking it within their practices. Consequently, the relationship with their ACP may feel more intimate and personal to patients, well beyond their medical symptoms and diagnoses. Last, in many practices, ACPs manage the day-to-day with regard to inpatient service or the relationship in the outpatient setting, where they may also see patients independently. In such cases, the physician (resident or attending) is a more transient provider of care and may change more frequently in either setting. This lends itself to patients perceiving the ACP as the most consistent and present member of their care team.

Working with hospital administrators

Our ACP courses also provided opportunities to work with colleagues in the healthcare organization who did not see patients. One group in particular that was eager to participate was hospital administrators. We have had regional hospital vice presidents and CFOs who were very curious about the course and wanted to experience for themselves what their clinical teams were doing. After participating, many expressed experiencing benefits from the course, although they found the skills practice portion challenging. This is a good example of how relationship-centered communication skills can expand beyond the patient-clinician interaction. This we accepted as a challenge and opportunity to make the course even better by adapting the skills practice session for comfort and applicability for such nonpatient care roles.

During one course, we asked one of the hospital administrators to identify his most common communication challenge that he would be willing to work on. He shared that talking to physicians about rules or policies was the most challenging. He gave an example in which he had to inform a surgeon that he could not travel to a lecture without obtaining approval from his chairman. He shared that he became extremely anxious in anticipation of such interactions and that they always ended terribly, with physicians storming out. He would "hold his breath" throughout the entire conversation, bracing for the worst. Not surprisingly, he reported trying to rush through these encounters.

We ran the skills practice a few times to allow him to experiment with different approaches. At first, with him playing himself as the administrator, he seemed defensive and aggressive. He did most of the talking, avoided eye contact, ignored the surgeon's reaction and emotions, cut the surgeon off each time he began to respond, and ended the interaction abruptly. He then switched into the physician role. After hearing his own words spoken to him, he articulated a greater awareness of his own style and developed more effective language. "That doesn't feel so good" or "I never realized" are common reflections after switching roles.

Thinking about this more broadly, relationships certainly aren't limited to healthcare, and effective techniques work in healthcare administration and leadership as well. This experience reaffirmed for us how powerful the relationship-centered techniques can be and how easily they apply to all types of communication interactions.

Every Word, Every Decision Matters

When considering which ACPs would be appropriate for relationship-centered communication training, we realized we needed to replace the references to a specific type of provider with the generic terms *provider, caregiver,* or *clinician.* This broadened the description and included others who might want to participate and allowed us to reduce the focus on particular academic degrees. We also added a point about the applicability of relationship-centered communication skills to contexts beyond the clinician-patient interaction (e.g., colleague to colleague, with family members, etc.). Helping providers to see that the skills transcend the patient-clinician encounter increased buy-in. In addition, we explicitly gave permission to participants not to do a traditional medical interview. If a clinician is not accustomed to using the traditional medical interview, the training session is not the time to start. Adapting the skills to how you have been trained to do the initial interview is critical. When we worked with standardized patients, we developed a case with the potential for various primary medical concerns, including psychosocial issues, in the hope of better generalizing the case to a large number of disciplines (e.g., social workers, dieticians, nurse educators, physician assistants, and clinical nurse practitioners). When we worked without standardized patients, we had the participants develop their own cases to make them relevant to their own experiences. In relationship-centered communication skills training, there is much more that binds us together than pulls us apart. Attending to the key issues of safety, respect, and learner-centeredness allowed us to work effectively on universal healthcare communication challenges.

Power Points

1. Stay relevant. We started with physicians because we knew that they hadn't been exposed to communication skills training as staff, and we wanted them to model the skills with their teams and with colleagues. As culture evolved, so did the training.

2. Be creative and flexible with the program content, depending on the diversity of your audience.

3. Appreciate differences in emphasis on communication skills throughout training for physicians and ACPs.

4. Know your environment. Deciding whether your culture is conducive or detrimental to integrated training from the outset is critical to protecting the safety of your learners.

Empathic Communication Through the Loop Lens

A Surgeon's Perspective

> *For this is the great error of our day in the treatment of the human body, that physicians separate the soul from the body.*[1]
>
> —SOCRATES

D r. Adrienne Boissy writes:

We knew early on that a communication skills program that was built and rolled out in a healthcare system that was largely run by surgeons needed not only surgeon input into content, but surgeon facilitators. People would make assumptions about "the type of person who teaches communication skills" and we wanted to highlight those assumptions and then squash them.

With some anxiety, we approached surgeons one by one and invited them to join our work. This was couched as, "We need your help. Surgeons are a huge part of the organization. You are well respected in the field, and we don't want a program to move forward without making sure we capture your voice." The overwhelming response to this approach was "OK." We wondered what we had been so afraid of.

Benzel was one of the first surgeons that we thought of and one of the first to come onboard.

Hog-tied. That's how I (Edward Benzel) initially felt about my involvement in facilitation training. I used that phrase liberally. Dr. Boissy had approached me about becoming a facilitator while I was the chairman of Neurosurgery. I responded that I thought there was a young female neuro-surgeon who had just joined the clinic who might be ideal. Boissy and my institute chair pushed back, saying that having the younger, less experienced female surgeon sent a message. Perhaps a message we don't usually talk about: that communication skills training is a gentle, feminine matter. Ultimately, I dove in.

I often hear that there is trepidation about approaching surgeons to participate in communication skills training. Surgeons have long been represented as aloof, highly intelligent, disconnected people. Look no further than the movies or TV. This was encapsulated by William Hurt in the film *The Doctor*: "I'd rather you cut straighter and cared less." There is no question about the importance of surgeons' technical skills. Who wants to suffer or die from unnecessary surgical complications? However, the dichotomy that implies that we must choose surgeons who are either technically skilled or empathic is a false one. Do you want an airplane pilot who knows how to take off or one who knows how to land? Is it too much to ask for both? Why can't we expect surgeons to be able to operate and to communicate? Strong communication skills are critical to a surgeon's work. They help in obtaining an accurate and complete history, educating the patient about treatment options, obtaining informed consent, helping the patient to understand the care plan, reducing patient complaints, and lowering the risk of malpractice suits. Medical and surgical colleagues face similar challenges, but some communication challenges have a unique flavor in the surgical setting—error disclosures, discussions about surgical complications, and at times, unexpected death at the surgeon's hands. One of the toughest conversations that we surgeons have is about what we are not going to do: "We are not going to perform your fifth back surgery for chronic pain." Sometimes the best thing we can do for a patient is not do anything at all, and it's a conversation we've never been taught. If we rely purely on our surgical techniques, what do we do when they aren't needed?

The Culture of Surgery

The fundamental role of the surgeon is to "heal with a knife"—to "fix" things. The healing process, however, extends far beyond the operating room. It begins with the first and ends with the last interaction between the two parties. It may, in fact, last a lifetime. The bond between a physician and patient has been recognized and cherished for millennia. Socrates was well aware of the importance of this bond and of the importance of considering the patient as a person with feelings and emotions.[2] The bond between the physician and patient is, in part, based on a commitment of the physician both to heal and to comfort.

If it's true that the "fixing" culture of healthcare gets in the way of relationship-centered communication, what might get in the way of surgeons comforting patients and attending to the more humanistic sides of medicine? Surgeons are thrill seekers. One of the main differences between surgeons and our medical counterparts is the appeal to the surgeon of the thrill associated with action. We surgeons perceive ourselves as doers and fixers. The appeal of doing and of fixing what is broken draws medical students to the surgical specialties. This macho aspect of surgery, in many regards, is fostered and nurtured in both the training and clinical practice environments. For example, the surgeon who swoops in to save the patient in an emergency situation feels the rush associated with swift and definitive action and is viewed, to some degree, as a hero.

Inarguably, the healing component of surgery requires technical surgical skills coupled with medical judgment, yet these same skills are insufficient for the comforting component of the bond between the surgeon and the patient. Sadness, anger, fear, and uncertainty are not amenable to being fixed. Emotional distress cannot be sutured, yet its expression is usually therapeutic. A very different constellation of skills is required for this component, in particular empathic communication and listening.

Our Experience Training Surgeons in Communication Skills

Having decided that surgeons and physicians alike would benefit from communication skills training, we faced the challenge of getting surgical buy-in. As in most hospitals, our surgeons are busy. The request of a full-day commitment to work on the development of more effective ways to communicate with patients risked provoking enormous backlash. The leadership of the communication skills training team used several key strategies to anticipate and reduce resistance: all the facilitators had a substantial active clinical practice, the message to participants focused on improving the experience of both clinicians and patients, physicians were placed in physician-only groups to increase a sense of safety, and they recruited senior surgeons as facilitators. These surgeons' humility and willingness to open themselves to the process sent ripples throughout the organization.

At a very basic level, when the course was being facilitated by a prominent urological surgeon, colorectal surgeon, thoracic surgeon, or neurosurgeon, it became more difficult for participants to argue that they didn't have time to participate or that the subject matter was irrelevant for surgeons. The fact that the CEO of our organization, a retired cardiac surgeon, had taken our course similarly supported our message that communication training was important and worthy of the time spent for *all* clinicians.

When we say we have surgeon facilitators, people look at us as though we stole the moon. Their disbelief seems rooted in the perception that surgeons are difficult to work with in the area of communication skills training. However, we found the perception of surgeons as uncaring technicians disinterested in empathy to be largely folklore. Surgeons were receptive and open to changing and improving their communication behaviors. They appreciated and embraced the importance of self-improvement. If more effective patient communication skills existed, surgeons appeared eager to learn and adapt them, just as they would want to master a new or improved surgical technique. One of the surgeons said, "I've been waiting my whole life for someone to tell me what I should say in this moment." This reinforced to us that healthcare is rich with difficult communication challenges, and clinicians do not always know what to say; they need the actual words and phrases. In addition, whereas internists and subspecialists in medicine who participated in our course enjoyed debating the relative merits of a variety of approaches, our surgical colleagues tended to appreciate and accept the fact that the facilitators had spent more time than they had thinking about communication with patients. The surgeons more readily focused on developing an understanding of and mastering the skills presented.

While surgical culture and training have not emphasized communication skills historically, our experience has been that surgeons are no less willing to work on these skills than other physicians if they are approached in a thoughtful and well-considered manner that takes into account their environment, culture, and experience.

Connecting the Ability to Communicate Effectively to Leadership

Leadership is the art of causing others to deliberately create a result that otherwise would not have happened.

—ANONYMOUS

All humans lead. An individual influences another by employing leadership skills, which is of particular relevance to surgeons. The expectations of surgeons as leaders are higher than for most professions. Surgeons lead teams that perform highly technical and orchestrated tasks. The successful completion of such tasks requires teamwork, a high level of organization, and guidance by an accomplished and skilled leader—the surgeon in the operating room. Surgeons, unfortunately, often fall short of such high leadership expectations, particularly outside the operating room environment. Patient compliance with medications, exercise regimens, weight loss, and so on is notoriously suboptimal for all physician groups.[3] For some, it feels more authoritarian and, therefore, more familiar to stay the "leader" in patient interactions; the price paid is the comforting component of the relationship between the surgeon and the patient. Too often, interactions become so doctor-centered that the patient can't get a word in, is smothered by the physician's monologue, and understands and retains only a small fraction of the transmitted information.[4] This approach results in suboptimal communication.

The practice of medicine is much more complex than simply writing a prescription for the right medication or performing an operation well. If the patient does not take the medication or the operation is not followed by appropriate rehabilitation, the surgeon may be guilty, to one degree or another, of ineffective communication and, arguably, suboptimal care. We understand that in expanding this definition of our role, we are making people uncomfortable, but if your role as a physician is to fix, then who determines when what required fixing has been fixed?

Expertise and execution that is appropriate in the OR may be inadvertently carried over to the bedside. One may derive from this discussion that the surgeon is the patient's leader, and consequently, his or her role is to tell the patient what to do and how to do it. This, however, would be taking leadership in the wrong way: the surgeon playing a paternalistic, autocratic leader. Such a surgeon (or medicine specialist, for that matter) may see herself as a leader, but in fact she is functioning as a boss. In this context, the boss tells her constituency (the patient) what to do, while a leader "causes others to deliberately create a result that otherwise would not have happened"—she actively participates by pulling in the same direction as her constituents. To quote Teddy Roosevelt, "People ask the difference between a leader and a boss. . . . The leader leads, and the boss drives."[5] Furthermore, if the surgeon is the leader, then the patient also assumes a role, and most patients these days don't consider themselves followers.

Many surgeons function as bosses, rather than as leaders. The end result is that the patient is not seen as a partner in the process, but rather, as someone in need of being told what to do. This is the doctor-centered approach. Effective relationship building via the employment of effective communication causes patients to do something they otherwise might not have done—take their medicines, come to appointments—the very definition of leadership. This is nearly always achieved via the use of a collaborative decision-making process. In a sense, the surgeon, by employing such leadership skills, is attempting to cause patients to play more of a leadership role in their own lives by respecting their autonomy, engaging them in their own care, and forming strong patient-doctor relationships. So, in this sense, both the patient and the surgeon are leaders. This is a win-win situation and at the core of a relationship-centered approach.

There are lapses in communication with patients and lapses in communication and behavior among colleagues. Since 2009, all hospitals have been required to generate policies for disruptive physician behavior. An internal review of such cases in our organization found that although there were few cases, the vast majority of these were related to the behavior of male surgeons. In fact, even though at the time, surgeons made up 20 percent of the organization, they accounted for 60 percent of the reports of disruptive physician behavior. Even more fuel for the empathy-is-needed fire is that the root causes of these cases included dealing with stressful and emotional situations, fatigue, and burnout. How we communicate as surgeons affects our colleagues, our teams, and our patients, and it reflects our leadership ability.

Surgical Education

The traditional approach to surgical education, which began in the latter 1800s (the modern surgical era), emphasized the diagnostic and technical aspects of medical care, while deemphasizing humanistic aspects such as empathic communication. We all know or have heard of surgeons who were tyrants—great surgeons, but people who made patients and colleagues feel awful. Their understudies modeled themselves after their mentors and defined surgical culture. They threw scalpels, pushed interns' heads into the surgical field so they could see, and berated and humiliated nurses and innumerable others. Generations of surgeons were trained to be unfeeling. Surgeons were expected to operate and operate well—lives were at stake—but to be blunt, focused, and relatively noncommunicative. Times, however, are changing—and changing for the good.

The modern-day surgeon uses effective and empathic communication skills, including reflective listening, to enhance the diagnosis, treatment, and care of the patient. Of course the act of surgery is critical, but there is much more to an episode of surgical care than the operation, and it is no longer enough to do only the operation well. An operation should only be performed on a clinically appropriate patient and should be followed by a focus on the details that optimize recovery and functional improvement. Diagnostic acumen and accuracy and patient adherence can be enhanced by knowing the patient. There is only one way to know the patient, and that is via effective communication.[6]

Traditionally, leading from a surgeon's perspective was thought to be commensurate with surgical prowess. The authoritarian aspect of traditional surgical leadership and training can be stifling regarding the educational process and be a detriment to patient care. This is not simply because of the direct impact of a monarchical culture, but because of the fear it fosters. The Joint Commission has an entire campaign dedicated to speaking up because they know safety depends on it. Their research suggests that wrong site surgeries, also known as *never* events, occur because no one wants to tell the surgeon it's the wrong leg, not because no one noticed. How does that happen? It happens because other people are afraid of the wrath of one individual.

This is not to deny that respecting hierarchy in the operating room is important. Hierarchy and role clarity ensures that patient care is guided by an expert, the surgeon leader, who is empowered to maintain order by directing team-member activities toward the common goal of an optimal outcome. Interpersonal skills can be employed so that a strong team is created, while giving all team members, including the patient, a voice. The voice of all team members is critical in promoting a culture of safety and preventing medical harm. Surgeons who have strong listening skills are more likely to hear their team members and their patients, who often have important information to share. In contrast, when a surgeon throws an instrument on the floor, swears, yells, or is bitingly sarcastic to a nurse, technician, or anesthesiologist—events that anyone who has spent time in an operating room has probably witnessed—those actions are destructive to the team caring for the patient and jeopardize relationships. Fear replaces trust. Fear of angering the surgeon not only makes an authentic relationship impossible, it undermines patient safety. If decisions are made in an unhealthy environment in which fear prevails, then cover-ups occur, personnel are afraid to speak up on the patient's behalf, communication breaks down, and complications result. This is a conclusion well supported by data from The Joint Commission and mortality and morbidity conferences.

Empathy for the Surgeon May Become Empathy for the Patient

What is the role of empathy in surgery? Do patients even want empathy from their surgeons? Surgeons go where other physicians don't. We open the human body and delve into its interstices. In this regard, we are perceived by some as playing God. We are thrust into a position in which we risk harming the patient. An element of toughness is required of surgeons that is not necessarily expected of many others. The surgeon must cognitively separate himself from the patient's pain and create some emotional distance between the patient and himself in order to be truly effective. This may be what prevents us from seeking a relationship of meaning with our patients. A neurosurgery resident once remarked, "Yesterday I had to tell a surgical intern not to cry over a patient who had died on the table because we had to move on to the next patient." This may seem callous, but it is nothing more than a learned coping mechanism within a system. In fact, this ability may well have adaptive advantages when caring for patients with life-threatening emergencies. But is it the only or best way to cope in the long run? The same resident asked, "If the military has required debriefing sessions with soldiers, why don't we have this for surgeons?" We witness trauma day in and day out, some of which we ourselves have caused. The work we do leaves a mark on us and, in most healthcare environments, we don't have anywhere to go to process our experiences.

If we expect our surgeons to care effectively for patients in a deeply empathic way, why then don't we take care of our surgeons? What is often lacking is an expression of caring. Caring and the expression of caring are two distinct things. The behavioral component of empathy, the expression of caring—a kind word, a show of concern, a touch, the verbal articulation of what the other person is experiencing—this is the essence of empathy. One study reported that when presented with empathic opportunities, physicians only responded to 10 percent of them.[7] Missed opportunities include not acknowledging, inappropriate use of humor, denial, and ending the conversation.[8] Another study looked at what behaviors from surgeons led patients *not* to recommend them to others, and 52 percent of the time, interest in the patient as a person and appropriate explanation were lacking.[9] Patients respect surgeons who care. Patients listen to surgeons who care. Patients want to be cared for by surgeons who care. Patients will not appreciate that a surgeon cares, however, unless the surgeon *expresses* this care.

Listening as a Lost Art

Levinson et al. published a review of communication approaches in surgery. The paper confirms that, unfortunately, most surgeons spend their time in a visit—up to 60 percent—conveying biomedical information in a one-way direction, that closed-end questions are the overwhelming norm,[10] and that psychosocial aspects of a patient's care were rarely addressed, in one study only 3 percent of the time.[11] Multiple studies have suggested the need for surgeons to explore a patient's ability to cope with the surgery itself, as well as managing the recovery process.[12]

Surgeons, perhaps more than their medical counterparts, are prone to lecture to, rather than dialogue with, patients. Such monologues are not effective means of education, nor of transmitting information. Patients do not accurately retain the majority of the information spewed by the lecturing physician.[13] Dialogues, as opposed to monologues, are much more effective means of educating and conveying vital information. A dialogue with the patient facilitates patient interaction, participation, understanding, and adherence.

Relationship-Centered Communication

Isn't it the surgeon's job to remove the diseased body part or repair what's broken? As long as the operation is successful, why is a relationship necessary? Isn't a great surgical outcome enough? Indeed, in some circumstances, the answers to these questions may be yes—and in some cases the patient might agree. All that the patient wanted was to be fixed, like taking a shaky car to the shop to have the wheels balanced. The surgeon easily could just balance the wheels. But patients aren't cars. And thinking of surgeons as mechanics is reductive and is a disservice to all the skills and value they bring—or can bring—to the table. As the surgeon grows in mastery of the surgical technique, it will be the human dimension that will challenge, engage, and reward the surgeon for performing the same surgery well 30 years from now.

From a historical perspective, the surgeon-patient relationship is perhaps one of the most revered and honored. Harvey Cushing, the father of modern neurosurgery, repeatedly documented his relationships with patients and how meaningful these relationships were to him.[14] In an ideal relationship, both parties benefit. Effective communication, therefore, is not just for patient benefit. The surgeon can feel enriched and revitalized as well. In an environment wherein clinicians are suffering from burnout in record numbers, we are all asking the question of how to engage them and provide meaning. In large part, the answer is to create relationships that matter and have meaning. At the end of each workday, clinicians should feel like they did good for patients and, hence, for themselves. And if they couldn't do the good they wanted to or if something went wrong, then they have valuable relationships with their patients, the stakeholders, and their teams, who will support and forgive them.

Power Points

1. Provide surgeons with communication skills training. They need it just as much as their medical colleagues and should not be exempt.

2. Identify surgeon facilitators who not only have foundational skills in communication but also influence within the organization to get surgical buy-in.

3. Approach surgeon colleagues with the same empathy and relationship-centeredness as you bring to others. It will do wonders for engagement in your process.

4. Know the evidence. Evidence suggests that patients want their surgeons to express empathy and interest in them as persons, which has implications on whether they will recommend a surgeon to others.

5. Surgeons have power over the environment they create in the OR and at the bedside. Adapting communication skills to each setting is critical to relationship building, safety, and resilience.

"Trust Me, I'm A Doctor!"

Building, Supporting, and Maintaining Professionalism

Dr. X is a 53-year-old surgeon who is nationally recognized for his surgical skills and innovative surgical techniques. He is a top revenue producer in his department. Recently, reports have surfaced that he often fails to show up for mandatory huddles in the operating room and often curses at nurses for being incompetent. His patient communication scores are low. Patients comment that his listening skills are poor, and time spent with patients is short with no opportunity for them to ask questions.

Professionalism as an Emerging Concept

In light of this scenario, it isn't surprising that there is a renewed emphasis on professionalism in American medicine. In 2002, a Physician Charter on Medical Professionalism was published with wide endorsement from multiple medical organizations in the United States and Western Europe.[1] This document aimed to update the concept of professionalism and bring it in line with values of late twentieth-century medicine. The charter is based on three principles (social justice, patient welfare, and autonomy) and nine commitments, including honesty with patients, patient confidentiality, maintaining trust, and professional competence. Most medical schools now have an explicit emphasis on professionalism as a core competency that students must demonstrate prior to graduation. Similarly, in 2003, the Accreditation Council for Graduate Medical Education (ACGME) established professionalism as one of six required core competencies that every graduate medical education program is required to incorporate into training.[2] The other five are patient care, medical knowledge, practice-based learning and improvement, systems-based practice, and interpersonal skills and communication.

> Dr. X's behavior demonstrates a lapse in professionalism, is disruptive, and threatens the quality and safety of patient care. Poor communication skills are clearly part of his problem; however, a formal curriculum and training in communication skills was not included in his surgical residency. When medical students or residents exhibit poor communication skills that lead to lapses in professionalism, there are clear mechanisms for identification and remediation. For attending physicians, such as Dr. X, the path to reporting and remediation of professionalism lapses is often unclear.

The focus in the physician charter, and the ACGME competencies for medical schools and residency programs, is on the responsibilities of individual physicians to fulfill the obligations of a medical professional. Recently, the question of "organizational professionalism" has been raised.[3] Organizational professionalism recognizes the fact that there are important and systematic ways that organizations behave that are out of an individual's control but that nonetheless impact professional behavior.[4] Conceptually, there is increasing recognition that professionalism is more than a simple set of rules that medical professionals follow blindly, but is, rather, a complex interplay between individuals and the environments in which they work, or what has been termed a complex adaptive system.[5] Along with recognizing the importance of context and complexity, scholarship is emerging around the theme of relationship-centered care, the idea that the smallest unit of measure in understanding communication is the relationship, not the individual.[6] This view is an elaboration of the concept of patient-centered care, which takes into account patients' values, preferences, and goals. Patient- and relationship-centered care are essential to providing high-quality, safe care.[7]

At Cleveland Clinic, relationship-centered communication using the R.E.D.E. model is a critical resource and a programmatic thread woven into our efforts. The R.E.D.E. model is an example of organizational professionalism that works by providing every physician training in relationship-centered care, thereby giving them the tools to meet the expectation that they will demonstrate effective communication skills in the work environment. In other words, the R.E.D.E. model represents how we expect professionals in this organization to communicate. This chapter explores efforts to integrate relationship-centered communication and professionalism into our culture.

> Dr. X is not singled out as a poor performer but rather
> takes this training along with the rest of his colleagues.
> Although initially skeptical, Dr. X is engaged by skilled

facilitators who focus on the benefits of communication skills and peers he respects who are in his course. He leaves the course sensitized to the impact his communication behaviors have on others and commits to practicing and learning how to listen more effectively in his work with nurses and patients.

To Act as a Unit

Cleveland Clinic was founded in 1921 and was profoundly influenced by the experience of three of its four founders, who worked shoulder to shoulder providing medical care to wounded soldiers on the battlefields of France during World War I. The ability of strong individuals to come together and "act as a unit" in war led the founders to see the benefits of group versus individual practice. Our model, "to act as a unit," represents the core values of patient care, research, and education embodied in our credo, "to provide better care of the sick, investigation of their problems, and education of those who serve." Cleveland Clinic also embraces innovation and individualism, celebrating pioneering advances in medicine led by physicians who pushed the boundaries of practice.[8] The organization is now a large multispecialty practice that is recognized widely as providing the most technically advanced medical care for the sickest patients.

One of the unintended consequences of this emphasis on technical care, which largely paralleled the emphasis on science and technology from the mid-twentieth century onward, was that we paid less attention to the more humanistic and relationship-centered aspects of medical practice. Consequently, unintentionally, we may have embraced and reinforced individuals who were disruptive because their technical innovations were not matched with effective relationship skills. When reflecting on his own career, Cleveland

Clinic CEO Toby Cosgrove acknowledged that while innovating and mastering technical aspects of cardiac surgery, he did not fully appreciate the importance of developing relationships with his patients. He established the Office of Patient Experience to integrate empathy and humanism into our medical practice. In 2008, Cosgrove reorganized our clinical structure into institutes designed to align services with the care of patients as opposed to traditional academic departmental silos.[9]

The culture of individualism and innovation that has propelled our reputation has resulted in some cases in discounting or ignoring elements of professionalism. In the past, Cleveland Clinic may have tolerated and even defended some disruptive physician behavior (angry outbursts, mistreatment of patients or nurses, etc.) if the individual(s) involved exhibited technical expertise and/or were high revenue producers. Fortunately, with the new emphases on relationship-centered communication and improving organizational culture and professionalism, the identification, remediation, and/or dismissal of disruptive physicians from the medical staff is now more systematic, and the focus of a Clinicwide Physician Conduct Committee (PCC).[10] The PCC was developed in response to the Joint Commission sentinel event alert of 2008 that identified disruptive physician behavior as a factor undermining the culture of safety in hospitals.[11] Its primary objective is "to eliminate disruptive and inappropriate behavior involving members of the Professional Staff."

> Dr. X continues to struggle with his communication in the operating room. For physicians like him, with a long history of disruptive behavior, a single course, while helpful, is unlikely to deal with the root cause(s) of the problem. The head nurse in the operating room makes a confidential report to the PCC. A member of the PCC meets with

Dr. X. The focus is on validating the value Dr. X brings to the organization because of his technical skills and ability to manage complex problems. After the committee determines that there are no personal issues at play, Dr. X is referred to a surgeon colleague with advanced training in communication skills who acts as a peer coach.

Professionalism Begins in Earnest

Despite progress in changing the culture of practice through communication and conduct, there was still a gap in the area of medical professionalism. Professionalism currently has a prominent and defined role in training medical students, residents, and fellows at all academic medical centers, and we are no exception. What became apparent, however, was that we lacked any formal program in professionalism for members of our medical staff. In response, Cleveland Clinic formed a Professionalism Task Force in 2011. After a six-month study period, the task force issued a series of recommendations to senior leadership, which included the formation of a Professionalism Council to enhance professionalism across the organization. The task force also consulted experts with experience in the area of organizational professionalism and culture change[12] and was introduced to the method of appreciative inquiry (AI).[13] AI focuses on what is going well and gives life to an organization and asks how to get more of it, rather than focusing on what is wrong with an organization and how to fix it. AI has been used successfully in worldwide business settings and now in medical organizations.[14] We ran an early exercise in which all members of the task force were asked to tell a story about a time that they were at their best. Powerful stories emerged, including how the death of a child led to an organized effort to improve patient safety in pediatrics and how going above and beyond in the service of

Patients First translated to wonderful patient outcomes that provided meaning for our caregivers. Telling our stories as part of AI transformed the group from interested individuals into a cohesive team. The stories connected our caregivers. At the same time, we realized that the relationships among task force members were as important to the process of culture change as they were to the organization as a whole[15]—a theme that has been critical to the success of the communication skills training with R.E.D.E. After all, clinicians have relationships with their patients and each other, but they also have a relationship with the organization they work within.

Several months into the introduction of AI, the task force leadership presented its work to the chief of staff and senior administrators. Despite concerns that a "soft" approach would not sit well, the group decided to use a round of AI storytelling to explore its transformational power with executive leadership. They told several moving stories, including the following from a senior executive and neurosurgeon:

> Early in his career as a neurosurgeon, he was in the midst of a complex brain surgery when he found himself unable to identify normal anatomic landmarks and, in his words, became "disoriented" and unsure of how to proceed. As a new staff physician, he felt vulnerable—he didn't want to appear incompetent in front of the surgical team—but he also wanted to provide the best care possible for the patient. He decided to call the chair of Neurosurgery, who came directly to the OR and helped him complete the case. The patient did well. In retrospect, the support he felt from his chairman made the words "to act as a unit" a reality for him as a junior staff physician. He has vivid memories of this event to this day.

The engagement of the senior leadership team made it clear that the AI approach would have traction across the organization. Senior leadership immediately adopted the task force recommendations to create a Professionalism Council, which remains active.

Communication, AI, and storytelling are central to the work of the Professionalism Council and the goal of making our culture more relationship-centered. For example, the council offers the Dialogues in Professionalism series, in which caregivers share stories with one another in a safe, supportive atmosphere. In these hour-long sessions, the facilitators briefly outline the goals of the council, introduce the concept of AI, and ask participants to write a brief narrative about their personal experience of "professionalism at its best." With permission, participants share their stories, which are recorded on video and catalogued. As a result of these sessions, several caregivers are now involved in professionalism activities within their own institutes or with the council.

Council members also felt that it would be useful to better understand how key leaders experience or think about professionalism at the Clinic. Several members of the council sat down with institute chairs for semistructured interviews. They asked chairs about professionalism challenges and best practices to enhance professionalism. There were wide variations in leaders' ideas on defining professionalism, professional lapses, and remediation efforts. As might be expected, dealing effectively with disruptive behavior, workplace stress, and production pressures were common themes in professionalism lapses. Responses—such as "But he is a good guy" when asked about *never* events, or "This is absolutely ridiculous" when a new initiative was introduced—capture some of the subtleties and cultural realities that our own leadership feels at times.

The council believes that the integration of professionalism in the onboarding of new physicians is critical. Several senior members reflected that as the organization has grown, some of its traditions are fading or have disappeared

TABLE 11.1 **To Act as a Unit Professionalism Series**

1. Cleveland Clinic Heritage/Introduction to Professionalism
2. Education of Those Who Serve
3. Physician Support
4. Leadership
5. Quality and Safety
6. Interprofessionalism

altogether. For example, by tradition, if a primary care physician called a specialist with a request for a patient to be seen, the expected response from the specialist was that he or she would gladly see the patient immediately, that day. As time has become more precious and patient loads have increased, some felt that the tradition of collegiality and effective relationships among colleagues has suffered. At times, calling a consult became so difficult (due to disagreement on whether the consult was necessary) that consult pagers were used to minimize individual variation and response. The recording and playback of transfer calls also highlight the pressures that clinicians feel and how that impacts their willingness to bring in transfers. In response, council members organized To Act as a Unit: Professionalism at Cleveland Clinic (Table 11.1), a series of interactive sessions that includes a full day of the R.E.D.E. to Communicate: FHC program and six additional two- to four-hour sessions.

A key component of these sessions is allowing physicians from diverse parts of the organization to meet, share their stories of professionalism at its finest, and engage through a relationship-centered communication approach.

The general introduction courses on heritage typically have 40 to 60 participants seated at round tables. Faculty and participants begin with relationship building and then

---

TABLE 11.2 **Agenda for Session on Professionalism**

1. Introductions of faculty and participants
2. Introduction to professionalism: review of the Physician Charter
3. Appreciative Inquiry exercise
   a. Introduction to AI
   b. Videotapes of students and faculty sharing stories in prior
      AI sessions
   c. Pair up and describe to your partner a time in your career when
      you were at your best as a medical professional (small groups
      at tables)
4. Skills that enhance professional resilience
   a. Situational awareness
   b. Teamwork
c. Communication under stress
5. Case discussions of professionalism challenges
6. Appreciative check out

---

listen to an interactive presentation highlighting our heritage. Following the heritage presentation, one of the faculty introduces appreciative inquiry and shares an AI story to illustrate the process. Importantly, facilitators demonstrate their own vulnerability prior to asking any participant to do the same. Participants share a personal story of professionalism. One participant spoke of initially feeling dismissive of the description of our organization as a group practice that "acted as a unit." He came from a solo practice in another state where he hadn't taken a day off in over 20 years. Shortly after he joined Cleveland Clinic, one of his parents died unexpectedly. He experienced unconditional support from his new practice partners who gave him time to deal with his personal issues. In his story, he expressed deep gratitude and a clear understanding of the concept "to act as a unit."

Facilitators introduce situational awareness and communication under stress as tools that support professionalism.

Finally, participants share cases of professionalism challenges in small groups, and facilitators debrief and discuss common challenges with the large group. Cases focus on conflict between professional and personal obligations, the lack of appropriate expertise to provide care, and how to intervene with an impaired colleague. An example of the agenda for the professionalism course is shown in Table 11.2.

Other courses follow a similar interactive format. Participants discuss Dr. X and similar cases in the professionalism courses as part of onboarding. This enables new physicians to understand the value the organization places on relationship-centered care and the resources available to support these efforts.

Building Not Recreating

When thinking about professionalism, what worked well for us was that parallel efforts to train staff in communication skills were underway and ultimately touched all of the professional staff physicians and many advanced care providers. In addition, all caregivers had taken service excellence training in the form of the Respond with H.E.A.R.T. program. Learning occurs best when it builds on existing knowledge, so we reinforced communication skills and service excellence through professionalism efforts. Several of the facilitators of the R.E.D.E. courses lead and also serve on the council. Because professionalism and communication are intimately linked, we also have members of the council design and facilitate our advanced communication courses. Cross-pollination allows for a richer discussion of the issues and reinforces communication training in which significant organizational effort has been made.

Ongoing and future collaboration involves working toward developing an integrated model of support for

FIGURE 11.1 **Concept Map of Professionalism at Cleveland Clinic**

physicians, including advanced peer coaching for professional development, online mindfulness training, and coordination of various programs in a Professional Staff Resource Center. In addition, as we analyze engagement results for our physicians, designing strategies that deeply invest in our own caregivers will be needed to drive the caregiver experience and, as a result, the patient experience. The council developed a concept map summarizing the various dimensions of professionalism at Cleveland Clinic (Figure 11.1).

> Dr. X finished six months of peer coaching with a surgeon who is a trained communication skills peer coach. As a result, he gained new insights into himself and his behavior. He has also mastered new skills that allow him to be more effective without being disruptive in the operating room.

In response to a growing recognition of the need and importance of creating a culture of individual and organizational professionalism, the Clinic adopted relationship-centered communication and appreciative inquiry as foundational. Having a dual emphasis on individual and organizational professionalism promotes a culture that both values and respects the desire of patients to be known and understood by their providers, and also builds relationships among our caregivers. There is synergy between relationship-centered care and professionalism, and this powerful combination can be applied broadly. To quote a popular maxim of Francis Peabody, "The secret of the care of the patient is in caring for the patient."[16] We would add, "In an era of highly bureaucratized medicine, the secret of caring for patients is to create a culture of caring that rests on the twin pillars of professionalism and establishing meaningful relationships irrespective of boundaries, silos, and status."

Power Points

1. Connect the dots. Communication is core to professionalism.

2. Get ahead of the curve. Medical bodies have outlined communication as a core competency both in medical training and for practicing physicians.

3. Tie communication skills to sentinel events to broaden the impact of effective communication on safety and quality and build a case for the training.

4. Foster your skill set with appreciative inquiry, which focuses on drawing out stories and qualities that represent people at their finest.

5. Ground professionalism efforts in R.E.D.E. or other communication skills training to reinforce a common language and cross-pollinate facilitators to maximize this benefit.

The Awesome Power of Vulnerability

When you are the physician in the room,
you fill the space, but as a husband, you
are simply half of a patient.

—ANESTHESIOLOGY RESIDENT DESCRIBING
GOING TO OB APPOINTMENTS
WITH HIS WIFE

t is difficult for those who have worked so hard at perfecting
their medical knowledge to reflect on the fact that they are
not perfect at something—people who may be the only one
in their families to become a doctor, who are following in
their parent's footsteps, who spent 16 years training for the
moment when they are ultimately responsible for a patient.
Acknowledging that they may not be great at something goes
against their grain. And if we look to history, at times, keeping
patients alive required our full attention, and communication
skills probably mattered less to the patient than not dying.

TABLE 12.1 **Communication Dos and Don'ts**

Keep	Stop
Matching the gravitas of the emotion	Saying I understand before you actually understand
Expressing your intention of care and doing the right thing	Telling people not to worry
Being empathically curious	Missing emotional cues
Perceiving emotional cues	Using reassurance or data to allay fear
Saying you don't know when you don't	"Winging it" when it comes to challenging conversations

Yet today, patients expect both. They expect competent, high-quality medical care, and they expect a level of service that clinicians may or may not be used to providing.

We want to acknowledge the thousands of caregivers who opened themselves to this training and who taught us many of the lessons and insights we've shared. They opened themselves to a process that they were skeptical about at times and that perhaps went against their grain, but they did it anyway. We'd like to spend time on some of the recurring themes they taught us (Table 12.1).

Major Recurring Communication Themes

Matching the gravitas of the emotion

> DOCTOR: Hi, Mr. Smith, I'm Dr. Brown. I understand you are here for a biopsy. How are you?

> PATIENT: I'm a little nervous. My friend bled and died from this procedure.

DOCTOR: You're at the best place. Our complication rate is less than one percent.

PATIENT: OK.

DOCTOR: I see you are from Indiana.

This conversation elicits several observations: one is that we really like to respond to emotion with data. We suspect this comes from being uncomfortable and not knowing what to say, and then subsequently defaulting to what makes us more comfortable, which is medical knowledge and data. This is another good example of responding to emotion with not just information, but reassurance. And in most cases, the reassurance is premature. Patients need hope, and we desperately want to give it to them. But premature or inappropriate reassurance can feel to patients as if we are dismissing their concerns rather than trying to understand them. Halpern addresses this in an article about a rape victim whose anxiety about being tethered to an IV was not eased by the doctor's description of all the pain management options she would have with the IV.[1] In such cases, physician efforts to educate patients only succeed in isolating them.

In cases wherein the patient is calm, not experiencing distress, and understands the percentage risk, it can be effective to discuss quantitative outcomes, but when they are hijacked by their amygdala, rational assurances generally don't have the impact we want them to have.

> *When patients are in their emotional brain, they need emotional responses.*

Expressing intention

> DOCTOR: We need to talk about quitting smoking. We
> talked about this last time, and there hasn't been
> much progress.
>
> PATIENT: It's been hard since my mom died.
>
> DOCTOR: Well, if you don't quit, you are going to have
> another heart attack, and you might get lung cancer.

If we were to stop this skills practice and ask physicians what their intentions are, they would respond that they care about the patient. If this is the case, it is generally much more effective to say, "I am really worried about you. I don't want you to have another heart attack." Or, "You mentioned to me how much you want to quit smoking. I want to do everything I can to support you in that goal." Anything else feels like badgering, and badgering is not an effective way to change human behavior.

Replacing judgment with empathic curiosity

Empathic curiosity is best captured by our V.I.E.W. mnemonic. It's a state of curiosity in the clinician that generates comments such as, "I'm wondering if . . ." or "Tell me more . . ." or "Help me understand . . ." When faced with patient behaviors or decisions that make no sense to us, perhaps we can start by trying to understand the patients' perspectives before trying to change their actions or their minds.

A middle-aged male was admitted to our hospital with metastatic testicular cancer, a highly curable malignancy, but he refused to let his medical team start chemotherapy. The team tried to talk him into it for two days. When a new attending took over, the team greeted him with "Maybe you can persuade him to start chemotherapy." The attending asked the trainees what they knew about the patient. They replied that he was a middle-aged male with metastatic testis cancer who was refusing curative chemotherapy. The attending proposed finding out who this person was. Doing so revealed that his father was terminally ill and that his mother had interfered with the patient's care when his illness was being worked up, telling her son, "Jesus will cure you." The patient's ex-girlfriend had thrown him out recently and had told him that she was pregnant, and that she didn't know whether he was the father. The patient had a new girlfriend. He was wondering which of these two women would visit him in the hospital. If the new girlfriend came to visit, then he wanted to make sure he preserved his fertility so that he could have children with her. If the old girlfriend came, she was already pregnant, so fertility was less important to him. Taking the time to sit and listen to his story, to start to form a relationship, and to build some trust had an effect. The following day, he consented to beginning treatment. To us, the problem was simply that he had a deadly, but curable, cancer that needed treatment. To him, he was suddenly sick. He felt let down by his mother, father, and an ex-girlfriend; and he was scared and lonely, lying in a hospital bed, wondering who cared enough to visit him. To him, the cancer wasn't the most important issue. Taking the time to get to know him and to form a relationship was more effective than using logical argument to persuade him that chemotherapy was worthwhile. His cancer was cured, and he remains well today.

We have also repeatedly resisted the idea that difficult patients exist—you hear these words frequently in healthcare. We believe that if you were fighting a losing battle for your life, you might be "difficult," too. You might raise your voice and even yell. You might behave in ways that make people not want to go in your room. Or you might seem irrational as you struggled with strong emotions. As our program evolved, we carefully referred to difficult conversations or scenarios, but avoided labeling patients as difficult, crazy, or otherwise. Once we label patients, our lens becomes tainted, and we start to respond based on our expectations of how the patient will behave rather than to the patient's actual behavior—an unconscious bias. We search for clues that confirm the validity of our judgment and become less interested in data that contradicts it. Consistent curiosity is the only cure.

Perceiving emotional cues

Patients drop emotional cues all the time. These are flags that signal what is going on in the hidden self that requires exploration or encouragement to draw out. Our perception is that, for a variety of reasons, many clinicians' antennae for these cues are poorly tuned or have been turned off. To have empathy, we must perceive the emotional cue in order to respond appropriately to it.

DOCTOR: Why did they get the ultrasound?

PATIENT: I don't know . . . my husband and I want to have kids, so I am pretty worried.

DOCTOR: What's the pain like?

This type of exchange is well described by Suchman et al., who categorized such moments as empathic opportunities that should generate empathic responses on the part of clinicians. In reviewing videotapes of physicians, they found that most emotional cues were "allowed to . . . pass without acknowledgement" and there was a quick return to the prior topic, which was usually a diagnostic explanation by the doctor.[2] When this happens, the patient's emotional state is invisible to the clinician and the patient feels unseen.

What struck us is that lack of attention to emotional cues has been going on for a long time. Suchman and others wrote about this phenomenon in the 1990s. There is no great mystery to why physicians think they are effective communicators and why patients don't perceive them that way. The disconnect has to do with our inability to be fully present with patients, pick up their cues, and be willing and able to respond to them. In our experience, this issue underlies innumerable cases in which doctors don't understand why their patient satisfaction scores are low despite all the explaining and listening they feel that they do. The truth is they still don't *see* the patient.

Saying you don't know when you really don't

> PATIENT: I don't know. I had a friend who had bariatric surgery. I've also had diabetes my whole life. Will that get better with surgery?

> DOCTOR: We can't be completely certain. It's a confusing topic, even to doctors.

We suspect that, for most doctors and advanced care providers, saying they don't know something after years of schooling feels odd. Perhaps even wrong. However, we embrace it as a phrase that acknowledges that although we know a lot, we don't know everything. When used in this way, it can align the provider with the patient, convey the complexity of the issue, and humble the clinician in the patient's eyes. Simply put, if we don't know the answer, let's just say that.

Phrases to Consider Eliminating from Our Language as Caregivers

I understand

PATIENT: I've had nausea for ten years.

DOCTOR: I see. What else is bothering you?

PATIENT: I've also been fatigued for ten years. It's been awful.

DOCTOR: OK. I understand.

PATIENT: You don't understand. I've been feeling ill for years. I can't work full-time. It interferes with my family life. You have no idea what that's like!

Many a time we have heard the words "I understand." These words seem harmless enough. Our desire to understand our patients is a good thing. Yet we've noticed that often these words are used very early in the conversation with a patient, long before the clinician has taken any time to actually understand or imagine the patient's perspective. Even later on in encounters, to what extent can we truly understand what it's like to be the other person? Have we experienced what this person has? In the scenario above, the patient knows this and becomes angry when the physician claims to understand.

> *If we haven't taken the time to understand, then we don't and we shouldn't say that we do.*

Rather than routinely saying, "I understand," it is best to modify it so that understanding is a goal rather than something that has already been accomplished. This doctor recognized the communication misstep and followed the patient's expression as follows:

> DOCTOR: Of course you're right. I haven't walked in your shoes. I want to take the time to better understand so that I can help you.

When tempted to use the words "I understand," clinicians should instead go for the powerhouse statement above or others, such as "I want to understand," "Help me understand," "I can only begin to understand," or "I can only imagine." Similarly, it is very different to say "I understand that you feel overwhelmed" or "Your frustration is understandable" than to say "I understand how you feel."

Don't worry

In talking to an orthopedic surgeon, a patient's family members expressed that they were worried about the hematocrit and the bilirubin. The physician responded with "Don't worry, we've got it covered." The comment felt like a pat on the head and a dismissal, despite what was probably the surgeon's best intention to reassure the patient and family. In another instance, a patient with a solitary kidney who was preparing for thyroidectomy told his surgeon that he wanted to make sure that the surgery didn't injure his remaining kidney. The surgeon replied, "You don't need to worry about your kidney. What we need to worry about is your thyroid gland." The patient fired the surgeon and chose to have his surgery at a different hospital.

Telling human beings not to worry is a highly ineffective strategy for reducing worry and can weaken relationships. Patients and family members will worry about their loved ones. Worry is completely natural and should absolutely occur when a loved one is ill or has an upcoming medical procedure. Telling loved ones not to worry is the equivalent of telling a child who has broken his leg not to cry. It negates the emotion itself, feels patronizing to most patients, and misses an opportunity to better understand the emotion in a meaningful way. Moreover, worry may have rational components, but it is not an inherently rational state; explanations without empathy generally fall short. We clinicians are more effective if we lead with curiosity and try to understand the worry rather than shut it down.

While visiting a hospital in New York, I heard the following conversation:

PATIENT'S MOTHER: I'm nervous about lung infection.

DOCTOR: We didn't find anything. You're right, that's concerning. We'll see what happens, but I don't think we'll start antibiotics.

MOM: So you aren't going to start oxygen?

DOCTOR: No, I think we'll stay where we are.

MOM: So you'll come down slowly on the fentanyl drip?

When you reflect on this dialogue, the mom effectively named the emotion in her first two words. Although the clinician briefly acknowledged it, the mother kept asking specific questions as a result of her nervousness, and the clinician kept responding to them. This is a common scenario in which the patient is asking a series of questions, and the doctor responds to them one by one without stepping back to try and understand the emotion driving the inquiry. A statement like "As I'm listening to you, it sounds as though you are really worried about your son" might go a long way in making the mother feel seen.

Consider this similar example:

DOCTOR: What do you know about a brain aneurysm?

PATIENT: Not much. A vessel can burst in your head and you can die.

DOCTOR: You're right, but do you know what it actually means?

In the first example, the patient's mother named the emotion she was feeling. In the second, the patient told the provider the reason for his fear: death. We've noticed that the word "death" no longer gives many clinicians pause, but it should. The words "dying," "death," "killed," "suffering," and "devastated" are significant clues to the patient's emotional state and need to be addressed directly. When a patient asks, "Am I going to die?" or "How long have I got, Doc?" there is a literal meaning to the question, but there is also an emotional one. The patient isn't simply asking for a numerical time interval, he is expressing despair: "Am I really going to die? What about my children? How will I tell them? How will they cope with losing a parent so early in life? Will I be in pain? Will I suffer? I promised my spouse I would be with her, and now I'm leaving her as a single parent . . ." The time interval is not necessarily the most urgent issue in the patient's mind. If we answer emotionally laden questions literally without addressing the emotional content directly, either the emotions continue to surface or the patient shuts down. Conversely, if patients feel there is safety and a willingness to hear and listen, they are more likely to disclose their feelings, and a stronger, more effective relationship can be developed.[3]

At the core of the discrepancy between clinicians' perceptions that they spend time, listen, and explain well versus the patients' perceptions that their main emotions are being ignored is the ability to recognize emotional cues and respond to them empathically.

Relationship Building as a Stealth Strategy: Decompress, Reflect, and Connect

We've spent a lot of time talking about programmatic considerations and lessons about facilitating experienced clinicians. We've been working in communication skills training for several years. Although we are newbies to the field in many ways, we have accomplished a great deal that many other organizations have not yet been able to accomplish, which is to develop and roll out a communication skills program that touches all our staff physicians and hundreds of advanced care providers. The program was scaled rapidly, and we honed our messaging and strategy.

During this period, we ourselves changed. We ventured out thinking that we would teach communication skills, hoping people would pick up a thing or two, but as time went on, we stumbled upon something much bigger. We learned that what we were actually doing was building a community where one didn't exist, reinvigorating clinicians to find meaning in the care they provided to patients, and creating a space of healing for them as well—and we did it by leveraging an effective communication skills program. We also captured the significant impact of the program on validated metrics of empathy, patient satisfaction, and burnout for over 1,500 physicians.[4] These accomplishments distinguish us from other efforts out there and define what makes us successful in engaging clinicians.

Nearly everywhere you turn today, you hear about the significant degree to which clinicians are burned out. Their own humanity is being suffocated because they don't have time to eat lunch or exercise or take a deep breath for that matter. The *Wall Street Journal* article "Why Doctors Are Sick of Their Profession" explored this very issue. Suicide rates, depression, and substance abuse are prevalent among doctors. Yet in some ways, the doctor has fallen out of the "patient-centered" solution.

It began early. In our own experiences, this was reinforced in a variety of ways. Medical school interviewers ask about hypothetical medical cases and what one might do in them rather than about the very personal essay a candidate wrote. In addition, exams in medical school are all about minutiae, thus developing and encouraging our laser-focused, data-driven, left-side brains. When graduating from medical school, the term "delayed gratification" was used to describe what we shouldn't do, and yet, it's what we have seen modeled for us at every step of our professional development. Wait to take a vacation until after MCATs, wait to decide the fate of a relationship until after residency matching, wait to have kids until after residency. Work hard now so you will be successful later. "This is a good time to invest in my career. I'll have time to take care of myself once I've finished my training," we told ourselves. But it never gets less busy and the years slip by. The current state is to sacrifice everything, despite the fact that we are no longer waiting for anything. The relentless work habits and long hours of medical school and residency create behavioral norms that stay with us through our careers. Add all the other pressures for RVUs, clinical transformation, quality, safety, and experience, and it's no wonder clinicians are disconnected and disenfranchised. We essentially built a "how to disconnect from other humans" system, reinforced it every step of the way, and then are surprised when caregivers are disconnected.

> *What makes people resilient or what can reduce burnout in today's caregivers is allowing space for decompression, reflection, and connection.*

By connection, we mean connection to patients, each other, and purpose—your meaning as you define it. Some people naturally may be able to handle these stressors better and regularly practice mindfulness or yoga, but telling young working parents to go to art class or spend 30 minutes at the spa requires a support system, resources, and adequate reserves. Many haven't figured out how to manage the stress, and self-care can come at the cost of not spending time with family and feeling guilty about it. So if our caregivers can't figure it out on their own, how can we support them more effectively in the workplace? In addition, because many clinicians may not be receptive to such stress-reduction efforts (or balk at them), these must be designed to feel relevant to clinicians and be reinforced by the organization itself. Remember, if clinicians don't think they are burned out or believe that feeling burnout means they are wimpy, they are unlikely to show up for a class called Resilience Training. What we learned from running our R.E.D.E. to Communicate: FHC course (which had a title relatively unappealing to physicians) is that if an experience is designed from the ground up to be responsive to and respectful of clinicians' experience, participants generally feel grateful for having attended, even if they hadn't been looking forward to it. The course ended up being a stealth resilience effort that presented itself as relationship-centered communication skills training, and participants felt it even if they didn't recognize it as such.

> The training experience you created transcends any prior work in communication skills, and I am so grateful to have participated. The relationships and development of community among all of us cannot be overstated.
>
> —PHYSICIAN PARTICIPANT AND MEDICAL
> SCHOOL FACULTY MEMBER

The common highlight of participant feedback was the value of spending time with colleagues. We captured the significant, sustained decrease in burnout with surveys after the course, and the questions moving forward will be: How does this change over time? How can we better intervene for our colleagues at different stages in their careers? In the end, it wasn't just sitting in a room with colleagues. It was forming relationships with them: knowing someone you could call for a consult (or had been calling but never met), sharing stories of providing care and being cared for, and becoming part of something bigger than yourself—a community of caregivers. If we are thoughtful about curriculum design, we can deliver an experience that allows caregivers to feel safe to decompress, reflect, and connect.

> *Communication skills training between clinician and patient reinforced skills for a better patient experience and ultimately improved the clinician . . . the human experience.*

The Awesome Power of Vulnerability

I sat in plainclothes at the bedside of a patient who participated on the Neurological Institute Voice of the Patient Advisory Council. I had come in to see him after his fourth or fifth back surgery. Gordon was a director of safety and quality efforts at a local company, and his wife, Jody, was at his side. The origin of his back problems was uncertain, but over years of surgeries, the couple had grown close with their neurosurgeon and one of the facilitators of the course, Dr. Ed Benzel. On this occasion, Gordon was lying on a bed in a dim room a day or so after surgery. This day, however, was unlike any other. After this surgery, Gordon had lost the use of his legs. Gordon and Jody recounted the story of how Dr. Benzel had come out of the OR to tell Jody that Gordon couldn't move his legs. He had closed the surgical site on Gordon's back, realized Gordon couldn't move his legs, reopened his back, yet was unable to change the outcome, despite all his efforts. I managed to maintain my composure as I listened to the suffering of my dear friend. What hit me was when Jody recounted how Dr. Benzel came out of the OR, apologized to her, hugged her, and cried with her. Imagine the impact he made on them.

Contrast that scenario with the behavior of a resident coming into Gordon's room the next day to change his bandage. As I sat there in my plainclothes, I watched in horror as the resident barely introduced himself, dismissed Jody's suggestions for more bandages, and then asked Gordon to roll on his back and push with his legs in order to do so. The nursing staff intervened after seeing my face, and I later asked the resident to join me to discuss what had happened. When speaking about this experience, he became emotional and shared the embarrassment he felt. When asked what he thought had happened, he explained that he had been loaded with "tasks," was covering for a colleague, and came into the room without having read anything about the patient.

The very nature of what we do as healthcare clinicians requires us to have resilience. We can't cry after every sad patient encounter and be fully present for the next one. That said, the person in a patient gown who is on the threshold of walking or not, talking or not, seeing or not, breathing or not, dying or not warrants recognition and respect. The physician drowning in tasks will never be able to fully provide recognition and respect, much less meaning for anyone.

I recently attended the International Leadership Board. This is a gathering of individuals from across the globe who come together for philanthropy in healthcare. I was quite nervous about presenting to this group. As I formulated a presentation, I was encouraged by the great Stewart Kohl, CEO of Riverside Companies, to be myself and to tell a story about patient experience. I told my story, or rather my mother and father's story.

I showed a picture of my parents in their younger days. Despite knowing that my father had leukemia, they married and had two children, and my father managed to keep his sense of humor. For Halloween he threw a white sheet over his head and ran around calling himself a white blood cell, the kind that causes leukemia. When my mom went to visit him in the hospital, she would stare at the IVs and medications and feel small. One evening, my mom was sent home with assurances that everything would be OK. Just a few hours later, my father died alone in the hospital. Twenty years after my father died, I wrote a letter to the woman at the National Institutes of Health who had hired my father as a statistician despite knowing that he had a "preexisting illness." He had been rejected for employment time and time again. I thanked her for giving him a chance. I wasn't looking for a response. It was just something that I felt I needed to do to complete one part of my life's journey. Unexpectedly, she wrote me a beautiful letter explaining that she "always felt he didn't want anyone, including himself, [to] allow his illness to keep him from doing what he [most] wanted to do." My father's struggle with leukemia was wrapped in suffering and death. Yet his boss's insightful recognition of my father's goal to remain vibrant as long as possible was a gift I unwrapped years later. The lesson for me is that we all just want to be seen, valued, and embraced for who we truly are—a lesson that profoundly influences how I lead patient experience efforts at Cleveland Clinic. It was hard for me to keep it together as I told my story.

Later in the afternoon, Dr. Brian Donley, our new chief of staff, gave his presentation. His first slide was a picture of his parents. He spoke of how his mother, a nurse, and his father, a pharmacist, had shaped his life and values. Here we were as the faces of leadership presenting at a global conference, and unknowingly, both of us had led with stories rooted in relationship and wounds.

Later that evening, Mr. Story, a cowboy-boot–wearing Texan who owns a multimillion-dollar company, came up to me, grabbed me by the shoulders, and said, "What you did up there was fantastic. I couldn't have done it." In that moment, I appreciated that it takes guts to share your scars and that being vulnerable is the path to strong connection.

Vulnerability can make most people feel deeply uncomfortable. The words commonly used to describe effective leaders, such as "decisive," "fearless," and "strong" are seemingly in contrast with what it takes to be vulnerable. Wikipedia defines vulnerability as the inability to withstand a hostile environment. No wonder we consider it a weakness! It is the Achilles' heel of a warrior, the weak spot in the fortress wall. The word itself is derived from a Latin root that means "to wound" or "wounding."

What's so interesting about vulnerability is that showing our wounds on occasion is precisely what enables empathy and human connection. It allows others to see us as human beings who, like all human beings, are imperfect and suffer. The human condition is a vulnerable one, and if we only project confidence, strength, and success, we are inherently inauthentic. Acknowledging that sometimes we fail, sometimes we're wrong, sometimes we suffer, allows others to see us as real. Acknowledging vulnerability requires humility, courage, and strength. Even the fiercest of warriors needs that every once in a while.

There was a time when the perception was that leaders knew what was best for those they led. Sound similar to doctors knowing what's best for their patients? It should. But the future is relational leadership, one that requires humility, engages empathic communication, values the opinions of others, and recognizes the power of relationships and how they influence behavior. Leaders also have to make decisions and are held responsible for those decisions. It is a burden that leaders bear, not one necessarily greater than those of the people they serve, but a responsibility that differentiates leaders from others.

Please don't get us wrong. We're not encouraging leaders to walk around sharing their stories of failure and suffering in every meeting or staff presentation. This is not about wearing your heart on your sleeve; it's about being an authentic human being and recognizing how this can impact the people around you. We are simply suggesting that with the appropriate opportunity, a dose of vulnerability can be uniquely powerful.

Why is this relevant for this work?

> *Building a communication program requires a willingness to model the behaviors you are trying to teach both when leading and when facilitating.*

It's somewhat disingenuous to espouse these skills when teaching only to throw them out the window when interacting with colleagues or making a decision for an organization. If leaders show little empathy for and curiosity about the people they lead, then it is hypocritical for them to ask for more empathy for patients. Yet developing relationship-centered leadership presents a real challenge. If you invest in your team as individuals and actively encourage and grow relationships among team members, then the failures or missteps of any of the teammates can sometimes mean more. The failure becomes a collective failure, not that of the individual.

In facilitation, there are a few ways to approach vulnerability in a group. This is important to understand because if you are effective at creating a safe space, then vulnerability will come, and you should be prepared for it. If someone starts to cry in a session because the topic has hit too close to home or some other emotion wells up, interrupt the session and ask the person what is present for him or her in that moment. We've seen this work beautifully when the person feeling emotional was willing to give it voice, and the approach was gentle. At the same time, this strategy calls tremendous attention to the vulnerability of a member of the group who may or may not feel safe sharing an emotion. Consider instead the statement "I'm noticing that something has come up for you. I'm wondering if it's something you want to take a minute to discuss or if it would be more helpful to you to keep it private for now?" Statements like this give power to the vulnerable person in a moment when the person probably doesn't feel very powerful. Another option is to ignore the emotion in the moment and address it on a break. But this strategy runs the risk of modeling to the group a behavior we strongly discourage in clinical work: ignoring other people's feelings. Perhaps the most effective method we have come across was modeled by Walter Baile and Rebecca Walters. A facilitator unexpectedly became emotional when another person was describing the loss of a child. The story called forth the agony of losing her own child. She excused herself from the room. Shortly after she left, a member of the team described his shame at not having realized what he had brought up.

Rebecca and Walter asked the team who else felt shame or sadness for ever having inadvertently touched on the pain of another person. Everyone in the room raised a hand. It was a moment in which the vulnerability of the group member was validated, shared, and released from isolation. He did not carry the feelings of shame or guilt alone.

Amy Windover attended an improv workshop and taught us something she learned called the failure bow. In this exercise, you bring a group together, and participants take turns announcing what they have failed in before taking an enormous bow (or curtsy) to the applause of the room. The exercise sounds a bit silly, and yet prompts some reflection. When was the last time you took a failure bow? If you had to take one tomorrow, what would you say? And who would clap for you? Would your leadership team rally around you in a round of applause? The reason most of us probably don't take a failure bow is because of the shame of failure. We are pretty sure no one would be clapping. Yet if we expect to live a life with no failures, we will be continually surprised and disappointed.

Conclusion

We opened the first chapter with the story of how our CEO, Toby Cosgrove, was floored by a simple question from Harvard Business School student Kara. We discussed the inspirational leadership of former Chief Experience Officer Jim Merlino, whose father died within the very organization he stepped up to serve. We shared more stories from our staff. These are examples of caregivers who achieved mastery of the science and surgical technique who were also willing to attend to the soul of the patient. Their willingness to share their own stories of emotion led an entire organization to Patients First. This book is the story of how relationship-centered communication and empathy for patients, our colleagues, ourselves, as well as empathy in leadership and strategy, can transform an organization.

The authentic human state is one of vulnerability. The commitment to relationship-centered communication requires that clinicians move from watching the suffering from a distance to step into the suffering of the patient and perhaps at times ourselves. This shift is transformative for those who have managed to make it. The world of regulation and checkboxes will always swirl around us. We must define our own meaning. We must be grounded in vulnerability and emotion because *that* is the human experience.

Notes

Acknowledgments

1. Ronald S. Burt, *Brokerage and Closure: An Introduction to Social Capital* (Oxford: Oxford University Press, 2005).
2. Nicholas A. Christakis and James H. Fowler, *Connected: The Surprising Power of Our Social Networks and How They Shape Our Lives* (New York: Little, Brown, and Company, 2009).

Chapter 1

1. T. Cosgrove, *The Cleveland Clinic Way* (New York: McGraw-Hill, 2013).
2. A. Cirillo, "The New CEO—Chief Experience Officer," Health-Leaders Media, healthleadersmedia.com, 2007.
3. J. Merlino, *Service Fanatics* (New York: McGraw-Hill, 2014).
4. Cleveland Clinic, *Empathy: The Human Connection to Patient Care*, 2013, http://www.youtube.com/watch?v=cDDWvj_q-o8, accessed November 15, 2015.
5. M. Neumann, F. Edelhauser, D. Tauschel et al., "Empathy Decline and Its Reasons: A Systematic Review of Studies with Medical Students and Residents," *Academic Medicine* 86 (2011): 996–1009; M. Hojat, S. Mangione, T. J. Nasca et al., "An Empirical Study of Decline in Empathy in Medical School, *Medical Education* 38 (2014): 934–41; M. Hojat, M. J. Vergare, K. Maxwell et al., "The Devil Is in the Third Year: a Longitudinal Study of Erosion of Empathy in Medical School," *Academic Medicine* 84 (2009): 1182–91; D. C. Chen, D. S. Kirshenbaum, J. Yan et al., "Characterizing Changes in Student Empathy Throughout Medical School, *Medical Teacher* 34 (2012): 305–11.
6. Committee on Quality of Health Care in America, *Crossing the Quality Chasm* (Institute of Medicine, 2001).
7. D. M. Berwick, T. W. Nolan, and J. Whittington, "The Triple Aim: Care, Health, and Cost," *Health Affairs (Project Hope)* 27 (2008): 759–69.

8. D. A. Hanauer, K. Zheng, D. C. Singer et al., "Public Awareness, Perception, and Use of Online Physician Rating Sites," *Journal of the American Medical Association* 311 (2014): 734–35.

9. A. Gawande, "Personal Best," *New Yorker*, October 3, 2011, 44–53.

10. J. K. Rao, L.A. Anderson, T. S. Inui et al., "Communication Interventions Make a Difference in Conversations Between Physicians and Patients: A Systematic Review of the Evidence," *Medical Care* 45 (2007): 340–49; M. Berkhof, H. J. van Rijssen, A. J. Schellart et al., "Effective Training Strategies for Teaching Communication Skills to Physicians: An Overview of Systematic Reviews," *Patient Education and Counseling* 84 (2011): 152–62; L. B. Mauksch, D. C. Dugdale, S. Dodson et al., "Relationship, Communication, and Efficiency in the Medical Encounter: Creating a Clinical Model from a Literature Review," *Archives of Internal Medicine* 168 (2008): 1387–95; L. Fallowfield, V. Jenkins, V. Farewell, et al., "Enduring Impact of Communication Skills Training: Results of a 12-Month Follow-up," *British Journal of Cancer* 89 (2003): 1445–49.

11. S. D. Preston and F. B. de Waal, "Empathy: Its Ultimate and Proximate Bases," *The Behavioral and Brain Sciences* 25 (2002): 1–20, discussion 20–71; B. C. Bernhardt and T. Singer, "The Neural Basis of Empathy," *Annual Review of Neuroscience* 35 (2012): 1–23.

12. A. Verghese, "Culture Shock—Patient as Icon, Icon as Patient," *New England Journal of Medicine* 359 (2008): 2748–51.

13. A. R. Boissy, P. J. Ford, R. C. Edgell et al., "Ethics Consultations in Stroke and Neurological Disease: A 7-Year Retrospective Review," *Neurocritical Care* 9 (2008): 394–99.

Chapter 2

1. A. R. Boissy and P. J. Ford, "A Touch of MS: Therapeutic Mislabeling," *Neurology* 78 (2012): 1981–85.

2. Boissy, A., A. K. Windover, D. Bokar, M. Karafa, K. Neuendorf, R. M. Frankel, J. Merlino, and M. B. Rothberg. "Communication Skills Training for Physicians Improves Patient Satisfaction." [In Eng]. *J Gen Intern Med* (Feb 26 2016). doi:10.1007/s11606-016-3597-2.

3. H. T. Stelfox, T. K. Gandhi, E. J. Orav, et al., "The Relation of Patient Satisfaction with Complaints Against Physicians and Malpractice Lawsuits," *American Journal of Medicine* 118 (2005): 1126–33; F. Fullam, A. N. Garman, T. J. Johnson, et al., "The Use of Patient Satisfaction Surveys and Alternative Coding Procedures

to Predict Malpractice Risk," *Medical Care* 47 (2009): 553–59; N. Ambady, D. Laplante, T. Nguyen, et al., "Surgeons' Tone of Voice: A Clue to Malpractice History," *Surgery* 132 (2002): 5–9; W. Levinson, D. L .Roter, J. P. Mullooly et al., "Physician-Patient Communication. The Relationship with Malpractice Claims Among Primary Care Physicians and Surgeons," *JAMA: The Journal of the American Medical Association* 277 (1997): 553–59.

Chapter 3

1. P. G. Henwood and E. M. Altmaier, "Evaluating the Effectiveness of Communication Skills Training: A Review of Research," *Clinical Performance and Quality Health Care* 4 (1996): 154–58; J. K. Rao, L. A. Anderson, T. S. Inui et al., "Communication Interventions Make a Difference in Conversations Between Physicians and Patients: A Systematic Review of the Evidence," *Medical Care* 45 (2007): 340–49.

2. M. A. Stewart, "Effective Physician-Patient Communication and Health Outcomes: A Review," *CMAJ* 152 (1995): 1423–33; S. J. Griffin, A. L. Kinmonth, M. W. Veltman et al., "Effect on Health-Related Outcomes of Interventions to Alter the Interaction Between Patients and Practitioners: A Systematic Review of Trials," *Annals of Family Medicine* 2 (2004): 595–608.

3. T. Stein, R. M. Frankel, and E. Krupat, "Enhancing Clinician Communication Skills in a Large Healthcare Organization: A Longitudinal Case Study," *Patient Education and Counseling* 58 (2005): 4–12; S. Williams, J. Weinman, and J. Dale, "Doctor-Patient Communication and Patient Satisfaction: A Review," *Family Practice* 15 (1998): 480–92.

4. S. Smith, J. L. Hanson, L. R. Tewksbury et al., "Teaching Patient Communication Skills to Medical Students: A Review of Randomized Controlled Trials," *Evaluation & the Health Professions* 30 (2007): 3–21; M. Berkhof, H. J. van Rijssen, A. J. Schellart et al., "Effective Training Strategies for Teaching Communication Skills to Physicians: An Overview of Systematic Reviews," *Patient Education and Counseling* 84 (2011): 152–62; I. Merckaert, Y. Libert, and D. Razavi, "Communication Skills Training in Cancer Care: Where Are We and Where Are We Going?," *Current Opinion in Oncology* 17 (2005): 319–30.

5. Griffin et al., "Effect on Health-Related Outcomes of Interventions to Alter the Interaction Between Patients and Practitioners"; Berkhof, van Rijssen, and Schellart et al., "Effective Training Strategies for Teaching Communication Skills to Physicians"; Z.

Kelm, J. Womer, J. K. Walter et al., "Interventions to Cultivate Physician Empathy: A Systematic Review," *BMC Medical Education* 14 (2014): 219; R. L. Hulsman, W. J. Ros, J. A. Winnubst et al., "Teaching Clinically Experienced Physicians Communication Skills. A Review of Evaluation Studies," *Medical Education* 33 (1999): 655–68.

6. Berkhof et al., "Effective Training Strategies for Teaching Communication Skills to Physicians"; C. A. Moulton, D. Tabak, R. Kneebone et al., "Teaching Communication Skills Using the Integrated Procedural Performance Instrument (IPPI): A Randomized Controlled Trial," *American Journal of Surgery* 197 (2009): 113–18.

7. A. L. Suchman, K. Markakis, H. B. Beckman et al., "A Model of Empathic Communication in the Medical Interview," *JAMA: The Journal of the American Medical Association* 277 (1997): 678–82.

8. M. S. Knowles, E. F. Holton, R. A. Swanson, *The Adult Learner: The Definitive Classic in Adult Education and Human Resource Development*, 7th ed. (Amsterdam, Boston: Elsevier, 2011).

9. Berkhof, van Rijssen, Schellart et al., "Effective Training Strategies for Teaching Communication Skills to Physicians."

10. Ibid.

Chapter 4

1. A. L. Suchman and D. A. Matthews, "What Makes the Patient-Doctor Relationship Therapeutic? Exploring the Connexional Dimension of Medical Care," *Annals of Internal Medicine* 108 (1988): 125–30.

2. L. J. Cozolino, *The Neuroscience of Human Relationships: Attachment and the Developing Social Brain* (New York, London: Norton & Company, 2014).

3. Ibid.

4. Suchman and Matthews, "What Makes the Patient-Doctor Relationship Therapeutic?"; Z. Di Blasi, E. Harkness, E. Ernst et al., "Influence of Context Effects on Health Outcomes: A Systematic Review," *Lancet* 357 (2001): 757–62; J. C. Norcross, "Relationships That Work: Evidence-Based Responsiveness," 2001; J. M. Kelley, G. Kraft-Todd, L. Schapira et al., "The Influence of the Patient-Clinician Relationship on Healthcare Outcomes: A Systematic Review and Meta-Analysis of Randomized Controlled Trials," *PLOS ONE* 9 (2014): e94207.

5. A. L. Suchman and P. Williamson, "An Introduction to Relationship-Centered Care," in *Leading Change in Healthcare:*

Transforming Organizations Using Complexity, Positive Psychology and Relationship-Centered Care, eds. A. Suchman, D. Sluyter, and P. Williamson (London: Radcliffe Publishing, 2011); M. Schmid Mast, "Dominance and Gender in the Physician-Patient Interaction," *Journal of Men's Health & Gender* 1 (2004): 354–58.

6. J. E. Carrillo, A. R. Green, and J. R. Betancourt, "Cross-Cultural Primary Care: A Patient-Based Approach," *Annals of Internal Medicine* 130 (1999): 829–34; G. L. Engel, "The Need for a New Medical Model: A Challenge for Biomedicine," *Science* 196 (1977): 129–36; I. R. McWhinney, "Beyond Diagnosis: An Approach to the Integration of Behavioral Science and Clinical Medicine," *New England Journal of Medicine* 287 (1972): 384–87.

7. S. Garba, A. Ahmed, A. Mai et al., "Proliferations of Scientific Medical Journals: A Burden or a Blessing," *Oman Medical Journal* 25 (2010): 311–14.

8. P. G. Armour, "The Learning Edge," *Communications of the ACM* 49 (2006): 19; M. Csikszentmihalyi, *Flow: The Psychology of Optimal Experience*, 1st ed. (New York: Harper & Row, 1990).

9. Suchman and Matthews, "What Makes the Patient-Doctor Relationship Therapeutic?"; D. Roter, "The Enduring and Evolving Nature of the Patient-Physician Relationship," *Patient Education and Counseling* 39 (2000): 5–15.

10. Pew Health Professions Commission, C. P. Tresolini, *Health Professions Education and Relationship-Centered Care: Report* (San Francisco, CA: Pew Health Professions Commission, UCSF Center for the Health Professions, 1994).

11. M. C. Beach and T. Inui, Relationship-Centered Care Research Network, "Relationship-Centered Care: A Constructive Reframing," *Journal of General Internal Medicine* 21, suppl. 1 (2006): S3–8.

12. R. M. Epstein, P. Franks, K. Fiscella et al., "Measuring Patient-Centered Communication in Patient-Physician Consultations: Theoretical and Practical Issues," *Social Science & Medicine* 61 (2005): 1516–28.

13. R. L. Street Jr., G. Makoul, N. K. Arora et al., "How Does Communication Heal? Pathways Linking Clinician-Patient Communication to Health Outcomes," *Patient Education and Counseling* 74 (2009): 295–301.

14. A. Bandura, "Self-Efficacy: Toward a Unifying Theory of Behavioral Change," *Psychological Review* 84 (1977): 191–215, 1977.

15. Beach and Inui, "Relationship-Centered Care."

16. L. M. Ong, J. C. de Haes, A. M. Hoos et al., "Doctor-Patient Communication: A Review of the Literature," *Social Science &*

Medicine 40 (1995): 903–18; K. B. Zolnierek and M. R. Dimatteo, "Physician Communication and Patient Adherence to Treatment: A Meta-Analysis," *Medical Care* 47 (2009): 826–34; T. D. Molfenter and R. L. Brown, "Effects of Physician Communication and Family Hardiness on Patient Medication Regimen Beliefs and Adherence," *General Medicine* 2 (2014): 136.

17. L. B. Mauksch, D. C. Dugdale, S. Dodson et al., "Relationship, Communication, and Efficiency in the Medical Encounter: Creating a Clinical Model from a Literature Review," *Archives of Internal Medicine* 168 (2008): 1387–95.

18. V. F. Keller and J. G. Carroll, "A New Model for Physician-Patient Communication," *Patient Education and Counseling* 23 (1994): 131–40; S. M. Kurtz, J. Silverman, J. Draper et al., *Teaching and Learning Communication Skills in Medicine*, 2nd ed. (Oxford, San Francisco: Radcliffe Pub., 2005); R. M. Frankel and T. Stein, "Getting the Most Out of the Clinical Encounter: The Four Habits Model," *Journal of Medical Practice Management* 16 (2001): 184–91; G. Makoul, "The SEGUE Framework for Teaching and Assessing Communication Skills," *Patient Education and Counseling* 45 (2001): 23–34; R. C. Smith, *Patient-Centered Interviewing: An Evidence-Based Method* (Philadelphia: Lippincott Williams & Wilkins, 2002); S. A. Cole and J. Bird, *The Medical Interview: The Three-Function Approach* (Mosby, 2000); G. Makoul, "Essential Elements of Communication in Medical Encounters: The Kalamazoo Consensus Statement," *Academic Medicine* 76 (2001): 390–93.

19. M. C. Beach and T. Inui, Relationship-Centered Care Research Network, "Relationship-Centered Care: A Constructive Reframing," *Journal of General Internal Medicine* 21, suppl. 1 (2006): S3–8.

20. Beach and Inui, "Relationship-Centered Care."

21. J. M. Gottman and N. Silver, *The Seven Principles for Making Marriage Work* (New York: Crown Publishers, 1999).

22. M. Bar, M. Neta, and H. Linz, "Very First Impressions," *Emotion* 6 (2006): 269–78; W. F. Chaplin, J. B. Phillips, J. D. Brown et al, "Handshaking, Gender, Personality, and First Impressions," *Journal of Personality and Social Psychology* 79 (2000): 110–17; F. W. Platt, D. L. Gaspar, J. L. Coulehan et al., " 'Tell Me About Yourself': The Patient-Centered Interview," *Annals of Internal Medicine* 134 (2001): 1079–85; A. J. Barsky 3rd, "Hidden Reasons Some Patients Visit Doctors," *Annals of Internal Medicine* 94 (1981): 492–98; G. Makoul, A. Zick, and M. Green, "An

Evidence-Based Perspective on Greetings in Medical Encounters," *Archives of Internal Medicine* 167 (2007): 1172–76.

23. Chaplin et al., "Handshaking, Gender, Personality, and First Impressions"; Makoul, Zick, and Green, "An Evidence-Based Perspective on Greetings in Medical Encounters."

24. Platt et al., "Tell Me About Yourself."

25. J. Nystrup, J. H. Larsen, and O. Risor, "Developing Communication Skills for the General Practice Consultation Process," *Sultan Qaboos University Medical Journal* 10 (2010): 318–25; J. F. Middleton, R. K. McKinley, and C. L. Gillies, "Effect of Patient Completed Agenda Forms and Doctors' Education About the Agenda on the Outcome of Consultations: Randomised Controlled Trial," *BMJ: British Medical Association* 332 (2006): 1238–42; W. Langewitz, M. Denz, A. Keller et al., "Spontaneous Talking Time at Start of Consultation in Outpatient Clinic: Cohort Study," *BMJ: British Medical Association* 325 (2002): 682–83; R. J. Henbest, G. S. Fehrsen, "Patient-Centredness: Is It Applicable Outside the West? Its Measurement and Effect on Outcomes," *Family Practice* 9 (1992): 311–17.

26. P. A. Barrier, J. T. Li, and N. M. Jensen, "Two Words to Improve Physician-Patient Communication: What Else?," *Mayo Clinic Proceedings* 78 (2003): 211–14; J. Heritage, J. D. Robinson, M. N. Elliott et al., "Reducing Patients' Unmet Concerns in Primary Care: The Difference One Word Can Make," *Journal of General Internal Medicine* 22 (2007): 1429–33; L. H. Baker, D. O'Connell, and F. W. Platt, "'What Else?' Setting the Agenda for the Clinical Interview," *Annals of Internal Medicine* 143 (2005): 766–70.

27. Middleton, McKinley, and Gillies, "Effect of Patient Completed Agenda Forms and Doctors' Education."

28. P. Sankar and N. L. Jones, "To Tell or Not to Tell: Primary Care Patients' Disclosure Deliberations," *Archives of Internal Medicine* 165 (2005): 2378–83; R. C. Burack and R. R. Carpenter, "The Predictive Value of the Presenting Complaint," *Journal of Family Practice* 16 (1983): 749–54.

29. J. White, W. Levinson, and D, Roter, "'Oh, by the Way . . .': The Closing Moments of the Medical Visit," *Journal of General Internal Medicine* 9 (1994): 24–28.

30. R. S. Margalit, D. Roter, M. A. Dunevant et al., "Electronic Medical Record Use and Physician-Patient Communication: An Observational Study of Israeli Primary Care Encounters," *Patient Education and Counseling* 61 (2006): 134–41.

31. A. K. Windover, J. Harry Isaacson, Lily C. Pien, J. Merrell, and Amy S. Moore, *Relationship-Centered Healthcare Communication: An Advanced Topic Guide* (Createspace, 2014); P. Duke, R. M. Frankel, and S. Reis, "How to Integrate the Electronic Health Record and Patient-Centered Communication into the Medical Visit: A Skills-Based Approach," *Teaching and Learning in Medicine* 25 (2013): 358–65.
32. J. M. Morse, J. Bottorff, G. Anderson et al., "Beyond Empathy: Expanding Expressions of Caring," *Journal of Advanced Nursing* 53 (1991): 75–87.
33. A. L. Suchman, K. Markakis, H. B. Beckman et al., "A Model of Empathic Communication in the Medical Interview," *JAMA: The Journal of the American Medical Association* 277 (1997): 678–82.
34. D. S. Morse, E. A. Edwardsen, and H. S. Gordon, "Missed Opportunities for Interval Empathy in Lung Cancer Communication," *Archives of Internal Medicine* 168 (2008): 1853–58.
35. W. Levinson, R. Gorawara-Bhat, and J. Lamb, "A Study of Patient Clues and Physician Responses in Primary Care and Surgical Settings," *JAMA: The Journal of the American Medical Association* 284 (2000): 1021–27.
36. Barsky 3rd, "Hidden Reasons Some Patients Visit Doctors"; M. Hojat, D. Z. Louis, F. W. Markham et al., "Physicians' Empathy and Clinical Outcomes for Diabetic Patients," *Academic Medicine* 86 (2011): 359–64; F. Derksen, J. Bensing, and A. Lagro-Janssen, "Effectiveness of Empathy in General Practice: A Systematic Review," *British Journal of General Practice: The Journal of the Royal College of General Practitioners* 63 (2013): 76–84.
37. J. L. Coulehan, F. W. Platt, B. Egener et al., " 'Let Me See If I Have This Right . . .': Words That Help Build Empathy," *Annals of Internal Medicine* 135 (2001): 221–27; E. Rautalinko, H. O. Lisper, and B. Ekehammar, "Reflective Listening in Counseling: Effects of Training Time and Evaluator Social Skills," *American Journal of Psychotherapy* 61 (2007): 191–209; K. Tallman, T. Janisse, R. M. Frankel, S. H. Sung, E. Krupat, and J. T. Hsu, "Communication Practices of Physicians with High Patient-Satisfaction Ratings," *The Permanente Journal* 11 (2007): 19–29.
38. M. K. Marvel, R. M. Epstein, K. Flowers et al., "Soliciting the Patient's Agenda: Have We Improved?," *JAMA: The Journal of the American Medical Association* 281 (1999): 283–87; H. B. Beckman, R. M. Frankel, "The Effect of Physician Behavior on

the Collection of Data," *Annals of Internal Medicine* 101 (1984): 692–96.

39. K. Koppett, *Training to Imagine: Practical Improvisational Theatre Techniques for Trainers and Managers to Enhance Creativity, Teamwork, Leadership and Learning* (Sterling, VA: Stylus Pub., 2013).

40. W. W. Weston, J. B. Brown, and M. A. Stewart, "Patient-Centred Interviewing Part I: Understanding Patients' Experiences," *Canadian Family Physician* 35 (1989): 147–51.

41. Marvel et al., "Soliciting the Patient's Agenda"; Beckman and Frankel, "The Effect of Physician Behavior."

42. Weston, Brown, and Stewart, "Patient-Centred Interviewing Part I."

43. Carrillo, Green, and Betancourt, "Cross-Cultural Primary Care"; A. Kleinman, L. Eisenberg, and B. Good, "Culture, Illness, and Care: Clinical Lessons from Anthropologic and Cross-Cultural Research," *Annals of Internal Medicine* 88 (1978): 251–58.

44. B. Starfield, C. Wray, K. Hess et al., "The Influence of Patient-Practitioner Agreement on Outcome of Care," *American Journal of Public Health* 71 (1981): 127–31.

45. Ong et al., "Doctor-Patient Communication"; M. Heisler, R. R. Bouknight, R. A. Hayward et al., "The Relative Importance of Physician Communication, Participatory Decision Making, and Patient Understanding in Diabetes Self-Management," *Journal of General Internal Medicine* 17 (2002): 243–52.

46. Y. Schenker, A. Fernandez, R. Sudore et al., "Interventions to Improve Patient Comprehension in Informed Consent for Medical and Surgical Procedures: A Systematic Review," *Medical Decision Making: An International Journal of the Society for Medical Decision Making* 31 (2011): 151–73.

47. Street et al., "How Does Communication Heal?"; Heisler et al., "The Relative Importance of Physician Communication"; Schenker et al., "Interventions to Improve Patient Comprehension."

48. Heisler et al., "The Relative Importance of Physician Communication"; D. L. Roter, M. Stewart, S. M. Putnam et al., "Communication Patterns of Primary Care Physicians," *JAMA: The Journal of the American Medical Association* 277 (1997): 350–56; M. Stewart, J. B. Brown, A. Donner et al., "The Impact of Patient-Centered Care on Outcomes," *Journal of Family Practice* 49 (2000): 796–804.

49. W. R. Miller and S. Rollnick, *Motivational Interviewing: Preparing People for Change*, 2nd ed. (New York: Guilford Press, 2002).

50. Ong et al., "Doctor-Patient Communication"; Heisler et al., "The Relative Importance of Physician Communication"; Schenker et al., "Interventions to Improve Patient Comprehension."
51. D. Schillinger, J. Piette, K. Grumbach et al., "Closing the Loop: Physician Communication with Diabetic Patients Who Have Low Health Literacy," *Archives of Internal Medicine* 163 (2003): 83–90.
52. Schillinger et al., "Closing the Loop."
53. Ong et al., "Doctor-Patient Communication"; Heisler et al., "The Relative Importance of Physician Communication."
54. Schenker et al., "Interventions to Improve Patient Comprehension."

Chapter 5

1. A. H. Maslow, "A Theory of Human Motivation," *Psychological Review* 50 (1943): 370–96.
2. I. D. Yalom, *The Theory and Practice of Group Psychotherapy*, 4th ed. (New York: Basic Books, 1995).
3. A. Windover, A. Boissy, T. Rice, T. Gilligan, V. Velez, and J. Merlino, "The REDE Model of Healthcare Communication: Optimizing Relationship as a Therapeutic Agent," *Journal of Patient Experience* 1 (2014): 8–13.
4. B. S. Bloom, *Taxonomy of Educational Objectives: The Classification of Educational Goals*, 1st ed. (New York: Longmans, Green, 1956).
5. D. Kirkpatrick, "Great Ideas Revisited. Techniques for Evaluating Training Programs. Revisiting Kirkpatrick's Four-Level Model," *Training and Development* 50, no. 1 (1996): 54–59.
6. M. S. Knowles, E. F. Holton, and R. A. Swanson, *The Adult Learner: The Definitive Classic in Adult Education and Human Resource Development* (Boston: Elsevier, 2005).
7. M. Weimer, *Learner-Centered Teaching: Five Key Changes to Practice*, 2nd ed. (San Francisco, CA: Jossey-Bass, 2013).
8. W. R. Miller and S. Rollnick, *Motivational Interviewing: Preparing People for Change*, 2nd ed. (New York: Guilford Press, 2002).
9. P. A. Barrier, J. T. Li, and N. M. Jensen, "Two Words to Improve Physician-Patient Communication: What Else?," *Mayo Clinic Proceedings* 78 (2003): 211–14; J. Heritage, J. D. Robinson, M. N. Elliott et al., "Reducing Patients' Unmet Concerns in Primary Care: The Difference One Word Can Make," *Journal of General Internal Medicine* 22 (2007): 1429–33.

10. K. A. Ericsson, "Deliberate Practice and Acquisition of Expert Performance: A General Overview," *Academic Emergency Medicine* 15 (2008): 988–94.
11. A. Chapman, "Conscious Competence Learning Model Matrix," http://www.businessballs.com.
12. W. Taylor, "Medical Education Learning Cycle," 2007, http://www .businessballs.com/consciouscompetencelearningmodel.htm.
13. J. Luft, *Of Human Interaction* (Palo Alto, CA: National Press Books, 1969).
14. Services CfMM, *Hospital Consumer Assessment of Healthcare Providers and Systems (HCAHPS)* (Baltimore, MD: Agency for Healthcare Research and Quality).

Chapter 6

1. P. F. Ferrari, "The Neuroscience of Social Relations. A Comparative-Based Approach to Empathy and to the Capacity of Evaluating Others' Action Value," *Behaviour* 151 (2014): 297–313; B. C. Bernhardt and T. Singer, "The Neural Basis of Empathy," *Annual Review of Neuroscience* 35 (2012): 1–23; N. Danziger, I. Faillenot, and R. Peyron, "Can We Share a Pain We Never Felt? Neural Correlates of Empathy in Patients with Congenital Insensitivity to Pain," *Neuron* 61 (2009): 203–12.
2. B. Edwards and V. Clarke, "The Psychological Impact of a Cancer Diagnosis on Families: The Influence of Family Functioning and Patients' Illness Characteristics on Depression and Anxiety," *Psycho-oncology* 13 (2004): 562–76; Y. J. Hwu, "The Impact of Chronic Illness on Patients," *Rehabilitation Nursing: The Official Journal of the Association of Rehabilitation Nurses* 20 (1995): 221–25.
3. T. Wider, "The Positive Image of the Physician in American Cinema During the 1930s," *Journal of Popular Film and Television* 17, no. 4 (1990): 139–52.
4. G. Flores, "Mad Scientists, Compassionate Healers, and Greedy Egotists: The Portrayal of Physicians in the Movies," *Journal of the National Medical Association* 94 (2002): 635–58.
5. O. Karnieli-Miller, R. M. Frankel, and T. S. Inui, "Cloak of Compassion, or Evidence of Elitism? An Empirical Analysis of White Coat Ceremonies," *Medical Education* 47 (2013): 97–108; D. A. Nash, "On the Symbolism of the White Coat," *Journal of Dental Education* 78 (2014): 1589–92.
6. Working Party of the Royal College of Physicians, "Doctors in Society: Medical Professionalism in a Changing World," *Clinical Medicine* (London, England) 5 (2005): S5–40.

7. Nash, "On the Symbolism of the White Coat."
8. N. Mathers, N. Jones, and D. Hannay, "Heartsink Patients: A Study of Their General Practitioners," *The British Journal of General Practice: The Journal of the Royal College of General Practitioners* 45 (1995): 293–96.
9. N. J. Mathers and L. Gask, "Surviving the 'Heartsink' Experience," *Family Practice* 12 (1995): 176–83.
10. S. R. Hahn, "Physical Symptoms and Physician-Experienced Difficulty in the Physician-Patient Relationship," *Annals of Internal Medicine* 134 (2001): 897–904; P. G. An, J. S. Rabatin, L. B. Manwell et al., "Burden of Difficult Encounters in Primary Care: Data from the Minimizing Error, Maximizing Outcomes Study," *Archives of Internal Medicine* 169 (2009): 410–14; E. E. Krebs, J. M. Garrett, and T. R. Konrad, "The Difficult Doctor? Characteristics of Physicians Who Report Frustration with Patients: An Analysis of Survey Data," *BMC Health Services Research* 6 (2006): 128; K. Kroenke, "Unburdening the Difficult Clinical Encounter,"*Archives of Internal Medicine* 169 (2009): 333–34.
11. T. B. Wetterneck, M. Linzer, J. E. McMurray et al., "Worklife and Satisfaction of General Internists," *Archives of Internal Medicine* 162 (2002): 649–56.
12. C. Johnston, "Suicide Totals for MDs Sad Reminder of Stresses Facing Medicine, Conference Told," *CMAJ: Canadian Medical Association Journal (journal de l'Association medicale canadienne)* 155 (1996): 109–11; C. Reimer, S. Trinkaus, and H. B. Jurkat, "Suicidal Tendencies of Physicians—an Overview," *Psychiatrische Praxis* 32 (2005): 381–85; E. S. Schernhammer and G. A. Colditz, "Suicide Rates Among Physicians: A Quantitative and Gender Assessment (Meta-Analysis)," *The American Journal of Psychiatry* 161 (2004): 2295–302.
13. J. E. Groves, "Taking Care of the Hateful Patient," *New England Journal of Medicine* 298 (1978): 883–87.
14. W. F. Baile, L. De Panfilis, S. Tanzi et al., "Using Sociodrama and Psychodrama to Teach Communication in End-of-Life Care," *Journal of Palliative Medicine* 15 (2012): 1006–10; W. F. Baile and R. Walters, "Applying Sociodramatic Methods in Teaching Transition to Palliative Care," *Journal of Pain and Symptom Management* 45 (2013): 606–19.
15. E. Kübler-Ross, *Death: The Final Stage of Growth* (Englewood Cliffs, NJ: Prentice-Hall, 1975).
16. W. F. Baile, R. Buckman, R. Lenzi et al., "SPIKES—A Six-Step Protocol for Delivering Bad News: Application to the Patient with Cancer," *Oncologist* 5 (2000): 302–11.

Chapter 7

1. A. Gawande, "Personal Best," *New Yorker*, October 3, 2011, 44–53.
2. J. Passmore, Association for Coaching, *Excellence in Coaching: The Industry Guide*, 2nd ed. (London and Philadelphia: Kogan Page Limited, 2010).
3. Ibid.

Chapter 8

1. K. Sibille, A. Greene, and J. P. Bush, "Preparing Physicians for the 21st Century: Targeting Communication Skills and the Promotion of Health Behavior Change," *Annals of Behavioral Science and Medical Education* 16 (2010): 7–13.
2. M. Passiment, H. Sacks, and G. Huang, *Medical Simulation in Medical Education: Results of an AAMC Survey* (Washington, D.C.: Association of American Medical Colleges, 2011).
3. A. H. Maslow, "A Theory of Human Motivation," *Psychology Review* 50 (1943): 370–96; A. H. Maslow, *Toward a Psychology of Being* (D Van Nostrand Company, 1962).
4. Association of American Medical Colleges, "Applicants and Matriculants Data," Table 6: Age of Applicants to U.S. Medical Schools at Anticipated Matriculation by Sex and Race/Ethnicity, 2013–2014 and 2014–2015, AAMC, 2015.
5. United States Census Bureau, "Census Bureau Reports 'Delayer Boom' as More Educated Women Have Children Later," 2011.
6. J. Younglaus and J. A. Fresne, *Physician Education Debt and the Cost to Attend Medical School: 2012 Update* (Association of American Medical Colleges, 2013).
7. F. W. Hafferty, "Beyond Curriculum Reform: Confronting Medicine's Hidden Curriculum," *Academic Medicine* 73 (1998): 403–7.

Chapter 9

1. R. L. Hulsman, W. J. Ros, J. A. Winnubst et al., "Teaching Clinically Experienced Physicians Communication Skills. A Review of Evaluation Studies," *Medical Education* 33 (1999): 655–68.
2. K. Donelan, C. M. DesRoches, R. S. Dittus et al., "Perspectives of Physicians and Nurse Practitioners on Primary Care Practice," *New England Journal of Medicine* 368 (2013): 1898–906.
3. L. L. Schlitzkus, K. N. Vogt, M. E. Sullivan et al., "Workplace Bullying of General Surgery Residents by Nurses," *Journal of Surgical Education* 71 (2014): e149–54.

4. S. Simons, "Workplace Bullying Experienced by Massachusetts Registered Nurses and the Relationship to Intention to Leave the Organization," *ANS. Advances in Nursing Science* 31 (2008): E48–59.
5. N. Lipkin, *What Keeps Leaders Up at Night: Recognizing and Resolving Your Most Troubling Management Issues* (New York: AMACOM, 2013).
6. D. R. Bridges, R. A. Davidson, P. S. Odegard et al., "Interprofessional Collaboration: Three Best Practice Models of Interprofessional Education," *Medical Education Online* 16 (2011); M. Hammick, D. Freeth, I. Koppel et al., "A Best Evidence Systematic Review of Interprofessional Education: BEME Guide no. 9," *Medical Teacher* 29 (2007): 735–51.

Chapter 10

1. Plato, *Charmides, or Temperance*, trans. Benjamin Jowett, classics.mit.edu/Plato/charmides.html, accessed 2/4/2016..
2. Ibid.
3. R. P. Kessels, "Patients' Memory for Medical Information," *Journal of the Royal Society of Medicine* 96 (2003): 219–22; National Center for Education Statistics, *The Health Literacy of America's Adults: Results from the 2003 National Assessment of Adult Literacy* (U.S. Department of Education, 2006); N. S. Parikh, R. M. Parker, J. R. Nurss, D. W. Baker, and M. V. Williams, "Shame and Health Literacy: The Unspoken Connection," *Patient Education and Counseling* 27 (1996): 33–39; M. A. Stewart, "Effective Physician-Patient Communication and Health Outcomes: A Review," *CMAJ* 152 (1995): 1423–33.
4. W. Levinson and N. Chaumeton, "Communication Between Surgeons and Patients in Routine Office Visits," *Surgery* 125 (1999): 127–34; D. Schillinger, J. Piete, K. Grumbach, F. Wang, C. Wilson, C. Daher, K. Leong-Grotz, C. Castro, and A. Bindman, "Closing the Loop: Physician Communication with Diabetic Patients Who Have Low Health Literacy," *Archives of Internal Medicine* 163 (2003): 83–90.
5. Theodore Roosevelt, "Quotation by Theodore Roosevelt," Dictionary.com, 1910, http://quotes.dictionary.com, accessed April 28, 2015.
6. K. A. Ericsson, "Deliberate Practice and Acquisition of Expert Performance: A General Overview," *Academic Emergency Medicine* 15 (2008): 988–94; M. Heisler, R. R. Bouknight, R. A. Hayward, D. M. Smith, and E. A. Kerr, "The Relative Importance

of Physician Communication, Participatory Decision Making, and Patient Understanding in Diabetes Self-Management," *Journal of General Internal Medicine* 17 (2002), 243–52; M. Hojat, D. Z. Louis, F. W. Markham, R. Wender, C. Rabinowitz, and J. S. Gonnella, "Physicians' Empathy and Clinical Outcomes for Diabetic Patients," *Academic Medicine* 86 (2011): 359–64; F. W. Platt, D. L. Gaspar, J. L. Coulehan, L. Fox, A. J. Adler, W. W. Weston, R. C. Smith, and M. Stewart, " 'Tell Me About Yourself': The Patient-Centered Interview," *Annals of Internal Medicine* 134 (2001): 1079–85; Stewart, "Effective Physician-Patient Communication and Health Outcomes"; R. L. Street Jr., G. Makoul, N. K. Arora, and R. M. Epstein, "How Does Communication Heal? Pathways Linking Clinician-Patient Communication to Health Outcomes," *Patient Education and Counseling* 74 (2009): 295–301.

7. D. S. Morse, E. A. Edwardsen, and H. S. Gordon, "Missed Opportunities for Interval Empathy in Lung Cancer Communication," *Archives of Internal Medicine* 168 (2008): 1853–58.

8. W. Levinson, R. Gorawara-Bhat, and J. Lamb, "A Study of Patient Clues and Physician Responses in Primary Care and Surgical Settings," *JAMA: The Journal of the American Medical Association* 284 (2000): 1021–27; A. L. Suchman, K. Markakis, H. B. Beckman, and R. Frankel, "A Model of Empathic Communication in the Medical Interview," *JAMA: The Journal of the American Medical Association* 277 (1997): 678–82.

9. R. B. McLafferty, R. G. Williams, A. D. Lambert, and G. L. Dunnington, "Surgeon Communication Behaviors That Lead Patients to Not Recommend the Surgeon to Family Members or Friends: Analysis and Impact," *Surgery* 140 (2006): 616–22; discussion 22–24.

10. Levinson and Chaumeton, "Communication Between Surgeons and Patients in Routine Office Visits"; D. L. Roter, G. Geller, B. A. Bernhardt, S. M. Larson, and T. Doksum, "Effects of Obstetrician Gender on Communication and Patient Satisfaction," *Obstetrics & Gynecology* 93 (1999): 635–41.

11. A. M. van Dulmen, "Communication During Gynecological Out-Patient Encounters," *Journal of Psychosomatic Obstetrics & Gynecology* 20 (1999): 119–26.

12. P. L. Hudak, K. Armstrong, C. Braddock 3rd, R. M. Frankel, and W. Levinson, "Older Patients' Unexpressed Concerns About Orthopaedic Surgery," *The Journal of Bone and Joint Surgery, American volume* 90 (2008): 1427–35.

13. P. A. Barrier, J. T. Li, and N. M. Jensen, "Two Words to Improve Physician-Patient Communication: What Else?," *Mayo Clinic Proceedings* 78 (2003): 211–14; J. Heritage, J. D. Robinson, M. N. Elliott, M. Beckett, and M. Wilkes, "Reducing Patients' Unmet Concerns in Primary Care: The Difference One Word Can Make," *Journal of General Internal Medicine* 22 (2007): 1429–33; W. Langewitz, M. Denz, A. Keller, A. Kiss, S. Ruttimann, and B. Wossmer, "Spontaneous Talking Time at Start of Consultation in Outpatient Clinic: Cohort Study," *BMJ: British Medical Association* 325 (2002): 682–83; E. Rautalinko, H. O. Lisper, and B. Ekehammar, "Reflective Listening in Counseling: Effects of Training Time and Evaluator Social Skills," *American Journal of Psychotherapy* 61 (2007): 191–209.
14. Michael Bliss, *Harvey Cushing : A Life in Surgery* (New York: Oxford University Press, 2005), xii.

Chapter 11

1. ABIM Foundation, American Board of Internal Medicine, ACP-ASIM Foundation, American College of Physicians–American Society of Internal Medicine, European Federation of Internal Medicine, "Medical Professionalism in the New Millennium: A Physician Charter," *Annals of Internal Medicine* 136, no. 3 (February 5, 2002): 243–46.
2. Accreditation Council for Graduate Medical Education, *Common Program Requirements*, 2013, https://http://www.acgme .org/acgmeweb/Portals/0/PFAssets/ProgramRequirements /CPRs2013.pdf, accessed May 30, 2015.
3. C. S. Lesser, C. R. Lucey, B. Egener, C. H. Braddock 3rd, S. L. Linas, and W. A. Levinson, "Behavioral and Systems View of Professionalism," *JAMA: The Journal of the American Medical Association* 304, no. 24 (December 22, 2010): 2732–37.
4. B. Egener, "Addressing Physicians' Impaired Communication Skills," *Journal of General Internal Medicine* 23, no. 11 (November 2008): 1890–95.
5. M. K. Wynia, M. A. Papadakis, W. M. Sullivan, and F. W. Hafferty, "More Than a List of Values and Desired Behaviors: A Foundational Understanding of Medical Professionalism," *Academic Medicine* 89, no. 5 (May 2014): 712–14; C. Lucey, W. Souba, "Perspective: The Problem with the Problem of Professionalism," *Academic Medicine* 85, no. 6 (June 2010): 1018–24.
6. A. K. Windover, A. Boissy, T. W. Rice, T. Gilligan, V. J. Velez, and J. Merlino, "The REDE Model of Healthcare Communication:

Optimizing Relationships as Therapeutic Agents," *Journal of Patient Experience* 1, no. 1 (2014): 8–13.

7. Committee on Quality of Health Care in America, *Crossing the Quality Chasm: A New Health System for the 21st Century* (Institute of Medicine, 2001).

8. J. D. Clough, P. G. Studer, and S. Szilagyi, *To Act as a Unit: The Story of Cleveland Clinic*, 5th ed. (Cleveland, Ohio: Cleveland Clinic Foundation, 2011).

9. T. Cosgove, "A Healthcare Model for the 21st Century: Patient-Centered, Integrated Delivery Systems," *Group Practice Journal* 60, no. 3 (2011).

10. We thank Nicholas Smedira, MD, for his contribution to the background on the Physician Conduct Committee.

11. The Joint Commission, "Behaviors That Undermine a Culture of Safety," *Sentinel Event Alert* 40 (July 9, 2008): 1–3.

12. A. L. Suchman, P. R. Williamson, D. K. Litzelman et al., "Toward an Informal Curriculum That Teaches Professionalism. Transforming the Social Environment of a Medical School," *Journal of General Internal Medicine* 19, no. 5, pt. 2 (May 2004): 501–4; R. M. Frankel, "Professionalism," in M. Feldman and J. Christensen, eds., *Behavioral Medicine: A Primary Care Handbook*, 3rd ed. (Appleton and Lange, 2008), 424–430; A. H. Cottingham, A. L. Suchman, D. K. Litzelman et al., "Enhancing the Informal Curriculum of a Medical School: A Case Study in Organizational Culture Change," *Journal of General Internal Medicine* 23, no. 6 (June 2008): 715–22.

13. G. R. Bushe and A. F. Kassam, "When Is Appreciative Inquiry Transformational: A Meta-Case Analysis," *Journal of Applied Behavioral Science* 41, no. 2 (2005): 161–81; N. May, D. Becker, and R. M. Frankel, eds., *Appreciative Inquiry in Healthcare: Positive Questions to Bring out the Best* (Brunswick, OH: Crown Custom Publishing, 2011).

14. D. L. Cooperrider and D. K. Whitney, *Appreciative Inquiry: A Positive Revolution in Change*, 1st ed. (San Francisco, CA: Berrett-Koehler, 2005); M. Plews-Ogan, N. May, J. B. Schorling et al., "Appreciative Inquiry and Graduate Medical Education," *ACGME Bulletin*, November 5–8, 2007.

15. A. B. Williams, "On Parallel Process in Social Work Supervision," *Clinical Social Work Journal* 25, no. 4 (1997): 126–38.

16. F. W. Peabody, "A Medical Classic: The Care of the Patient by Francis W. Peabody," *Journal of American Medical Association*, 88 (1927): 877; *Medical Times* 101, no. 10 (October 1973): 62–64.

Chapter 12

1. J. Halpern, "What Is Clinical Empathy?," *Journal of General Internal Medicine* 18 (2003): 670–74.
2. A. L. Suchman, K. Markakis, H. B. Beckman et al., "A Model of Empathic Communication in the Medical Interview," *JAMA: The Journal of the American Medical Association* 277 (1997): 678–82.
3. L. Del Piccolo, O. Danzi, N. Fattori et al., "How Psychiatrist's Communication Skills and Patient's Diagnosis Affect Emotions Disclosure During First Diagnostic Consultations," *Patient Education and Counseling* 96 (2014): 151–58.
4. Boissy, A., A. K. Windover, D. Bokar, M. Karafa, K. Neuendorf, R. M. Frankel, J. Merlino, and M. B. Rothberg. "Communication Skills Training for Physicians Improves Patient Satisfaction." [In Eng]. *J Gen Intern Med* (Feb 26 2016). doi:10.1007/s11606-016-3597-2.

Index

About the Editors

Adrienne Boissy, MD, MA, is chief experience officer of Cleveland Clinic Health System and a staff neurologist at the Cleveland Clinic Mellen Center for Multiple Sclerosis. In this role, Dr. Boissy leads the Office of Patient Experience and its initiatives to address and improve every aspect of a patient's encounter with the Cleveland Clinic Health System—from patients' physical comfort to their educational, emotional, and spiritual needs. The Office of Patient Experience is responsible for a range of programs and services across the hospital, including service excellence, communication skills training, spiritual care, bioethics, data intelligence, volunteer services, and the ombudsman's office.

Dr. Boissy previously served as the medical director of the Center of Excellence in Healthcare Communication. Her team created a comprehensive program to strengthen physician and clinician communication skills throughout Cleveland Clinic and has trained thousands of staff physicians and clinicians to date.

Dr. Boissy chairs the Empathy and Innovation summit, the largest independent summit on patient experience in the world. She also guided the development of patient advisory councils across Cleveland Clinic Health System and currently serves as editor-in-chief of the *Journal of Patient Experience.*

In addition, Dr. Boissy was awarded an Arnold P. Gold Foundation grant for humanism in medicine. She continues to care for patients with multiple sclerosis and also serves on the editorial board of the National Multiple Sclerosis Society's *Momentum* magazine.

She has published extensively about relationships and empathy in healthcare and the communication challenges in clinical practice, which were highlighted in her 2015 TEDx talk "Seeing and Being Seen: A Call for Healing." Dr. Boissy is frequently interviewed in the media as an expert in patient experience, physician communication, and transparency. Her quotes have appeared in the *Wall Street Journal*, the *Washington Post*, *Forbes*, and the *Atlantic*, among others. A Harvard Macy scholar, she has spoken extensively around the country about the patient and provider experience and the impact of effective communication on both.

Dr. Boissy attended Boston University and worked in neurobiological research at Brigham and Women's Hospital, Boston. She completed her medical school training at Pennsylvania State University College of Medicine and finished her neurology residency and neuroimmunology fellowship at Cleveland Clinic.

imothy Gilligan, MD, MS, is the former co-director of the Cleveland Clinic Center for Excellence in Healthcare Communication (CEHC), where he teaches communication skills, trains others to teach communication skills, and provides physician coaching. He directs the innovative peer communication coaching program within CEHC and holds workshops on physician communication at national and international conferences. He has completed communication skills training in the Oncotalk Teach program and AACH Facilitator-in-Training program. He is currently an AACH faculty member.

Dr. Gilligan is Vice-Chair for Education at Cleveland Clinic's Taussig Cancer Institute and a medical oncologist specializing in cancers of the testicles, bladder, prostate, and kidneys. He is an associate professor of medicine at the Cleveland Clinic Lerner College of Medicine, with appointments in the departments of Hematology and Medical Oncology, Urology, and Bioethics.

Dr. Gilligan has published original scientific articles in peer-reviewed journals, written review articles and book chapters, and given lectures on genitourinary cancers and biomedical ethics. He has written and edited treatment guidelines and cancer information summaries for national and international organizations, including the National Cancer Institute, the American Society of Clinical Oncology, and UpToDate. He also works on quality initiatives with the American Society of Clinical Oncology (ASCO), for which he has served on the Quality of Care Committee, and chaired both the Subcommittee on Quality Measures and the Test Materials Development Committee. He is a faculty member of the ASCO Quality Training Program.

A graduate of Stanford University Medical School, Dr. Gilligan completed his residency in internal medicine and medical oncology at Brigham and Women's Hospital and his fellowship at the Dana-Farber Cancer Institute.

Put the Cleveland Clinic Way to Work for You

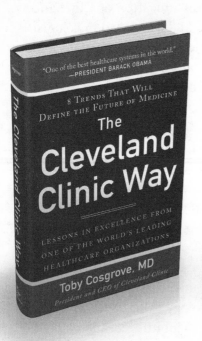

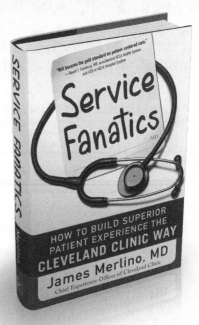

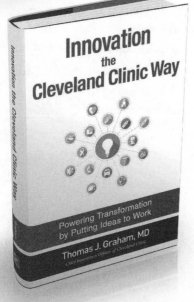

"Cleveland Clinic [is] one of the best healthcare systems in the world."

— President Barack Obama

"This is the story of one of the world's leading medical centers going through transformation without losing sight of its true mission."

— Alex Gorsky, Chairman and CEO of *Johnson & Johnson*